WICCA

About the Author

Scott Cunningham practiced elemental magic for over twenty years. He authored more than thirty books, both fiction and nonfiction. Scott's books reflect a broad range of interests from the New Age sphere, where he was highly regarded. He passed from this life on March 28, 1993, after a long illness.

WICCA

A GUIDE FOR THE SOLITARY PRACTITIONER

SCOTT CUNNINGHAM

Llewellyn Publications
Woodbury, Minnesota

FIRST EDITION, REVISED
Fifty-fifth Printing, 2021

Book design by Alexander Negrete and Kimberly Nightingale
Cover design by Anne Marie Garrison
Cover illustration © 2002 by Anthony Meadows
Interior illustrations by Kevin Brown
Revised edition edited by Kimberly Nightingale

Library of Congress Cataloging-in-Publication Data
Cunningham, Scott, 1956–1993
    Wicca: a guide for the solitary practitioner.
    Bibliography: p.
    1. Witchcraft. 2. Magic. 3. Ritual.
    I. Title. II. Series.
    BF1566.C86   1988   299   88–45279
    ISBN 13: 978-0-87542-118-6
    ISBN 10: 0-87542-118-0

Llewellyn Publications
A Division of Llewellyn Worldwide Ltd.
2143 Wooddale Drive
Woodbury, MN 55125-2989
www.llewellyn.com

Llewellyn is a registered trademark of Llewellyn Worldwide Ltd.

Printed in the United States of America

This book is dedicated to the forces that watch over and guide us—
however we may envision or name them.

Acknowledgments

To deTraci Regula, Marilee, Juanita, and Mark and Kyri of the Silver Wheel for commenting on earlier drafts of the work.

To Morgan, Morgana, Abraham, Barda, and all those who have shared their knowledge and practices with me.

To all my friends at Llewellyn for their years of continuing support.

Contents

Section I: Theory

Section II: Practice

Section III: The Standing Stones Book of Shadows

Preface

THIS BOOK, THE result of sixteen years of practical experience and research, is a guidebook outlining basic Wiccan theory and practice. It is written with the solitary student or practitioner in mind; there are no coven rituals or magical group dynamics described herein.

The Wicca as described here is "new." It is not a revelation of ancient rituals handed down for thousands of years. This does not invalidate it, however, for it is based on time-honored practices.

A three-thousand-year-old incantation to manna isn't necessarily more powerful or effective than one improvised during a private rite. The person practicing the ritual or spell determines its success.

If centuries-old incantations are nothing more to you than senseless gibberish, chances are the ritual won't work, any more than would a Shinto ceremony in the hands of a Methodist. To be effective, rituals must speak to you.

Rituals are at the heart of Wicca for some, and are pleasant adjuncts to Wicca's philosophy and way of life for others. In Wicca, as with every religion, ritual is a means of contacting the divine. Effective ritual unites the worshipper with deity. Ineffective ritual kills spirituality.

There are rituals in this book, yes, but they're guideposts, not holy writ. I wrote them so that others, using them as general guidelines, could create their own.

Some people might say, "But that's just your stuff. We want the *real* Wicca! *Tell us the secrets!*"

There is not, and can never be, one "pure" or "true" or "genuine" form of Wicca. There are no central governing agencies, no physical leaders, no universally recognized prophets or messengers. Although specific, structured forms of Wicca certainly exist, they aren't in agreement regarding ritual, symbolism, and theology. Because of this healthy individualism, no one ritual or philosophical system has emerged to consume the others.

Wicca is varied and multi-faceted. As in every religion, the Wiccan spiritual experience is one shared with deity alone. This book is simply one way, based on my experiences and the instruction I have received, to practice Wicca.

Although I wrote it, it didn't hatch out of thin air. The jeweler who facets rough emeralds didn't create the gemstones; nor the potter the clay. I've tried to present a blending of the major themes and ritual structures of Wicca, not to create a new form, but to present one so that others can develop their own Wiccan practices.

When I began learning Wicca there were few books, certainly no published Books of Shadows.* Wiccan rituals and magical texts are secret within many traditions of Wicca, and it wasn't until recently that any systems have "gone public." Due to this fact, few Wiccans wrote books describing the rituals and inner teachings of Wicca. Those outside the Wicca (or the Craft as it is also known) who wrote of it could necessarily report only garbled or incomplete pictures.

Within a few years of my introduction to Wicca, however, many authentic, informative books began to be published. As I continued my studies, both independently and under teachers I had met, I realized that anyone trying to learn and practice Wicca solely from published sources would gain a sadly unbalanced picture.

Most Wiccan authors tout their own form of Wicca. This makes sense: write what you know. Unfortunately, many of the foremost Wiccan authors share similar views, and so most of the published Wiccan material is repetitive.

Also, most of these books are geared toward coven-(group) oriented Wicca. This poses a problem for anyone unable to find a minimum of

---

* See glossary for unfamiliar terms.

four or five interested, compatible persons to create a coven. It also lays a burden on those who desire private religious practice.

Perhaps my true reason for writing this book—besides numerous requests—is strictly personal. I not only wish to present an alternate to staid, structured Wiccan books, I also want to return something for the training I have received in this contemporary religion.

Although I occasionally teach, and Wicca always draws a crowd, I prefer the medium of printed words to point out some of the things I have learned. Although nothing can replace one-on-one teaching, this isn't practical for all those desiring to learn.

And so, several years ago, I began jotting down notes and chapters that eventually became this book. To avoid becoming too narrow-minded (Sybil Leek once said that it was dangerous writing about your own religion—you're too close to it), I've had Wiccan friends read and comment on early drafts to ensure that the picture of Wicca presented here isn't too limited or dogmatic.

Please don't misunderstand me. Though this book's goal is a wider understanding of, and appreciation of Wicca, I'm not proselytizing. Like most Wiccans, I'm not out to change your spiritual and religious beliefs; it's none of my business.

However, with the continuing interest in nontraditional religions, concern over environmental destruction, and a wide interest in the Wiccan religion, I hope this book partially answers one of the questions I'm most commonly asked: "What is Wicca?"

Linguistic Note

Much disagreement concerning the exact (and original) meaning of the word "Wicca" presently exists. It's not my intention to enter into or add to such discussions, but I don't feel that I can use this term without defining it. Therefore, "Wicca" will be used within this book to describe both the religion itself (a loosely organized pagan religion centering toward reverence for the creative forces of nature, usually symbolized by a goddess and a god), as well as its practitioners of both sexes. The term "Warlock," though sometimes used to describe male practitioners, is virtually never used by Wiccans themselves; hence I've avoided it here. Though some use "Wicca" and "Witch" almost interchangeably, I prefer the older, less-encumbered word "Wicca," and so use it almost exclusively.

Introduction

WICCA, THE RELIGION of the "Witches," has long been shrouded in secrecy. Anyone interested in learning "the Craft" had to content themselves with hints from books and articles. The Wiccans wouldn't say much, save that they weren't looking for new members.

Growing numbers of people today are dissatisfied with traditional religious structures. Many are searching for a personally involving religion, one that celebrates both physical and spiritual realities, in which attunement with deity is coupled with the practice of magic.

Wicca is just such a religion, centering around reverence for nature as seen in the Goddess and the God. Its spiritual roots in antiquity, acceptance of magic, and mysterious nature have made it particularly appealing. Until recently, the lack of public information concerning Wicca and its apparent exclusivity has caused much frustration among interested students.

Wicca doesn't seek new members. This has been a major stumbling block to those wishing to learn its rites and ways of magic. Wicca doesn't solicit because, unlike most western religions, it doesn't claim to be the one true way to deity.

With growing numbers interested in practicing Wicca, perhaps it's time to allow the full light of the dawning Aquarian Age to illuminate these ways. To do so is not to trumpet Wicca as the salvation of our planet, but simply to present it to anyone who cares to learn.

There have been many obstacles. In the past the only way to enter Wicca was to a) contact an initiated Wicca, usually a coven member, and b) receive initiation. If you didn't know any Witches you were out of luck, for initiation was an absolute prerequisite.

Today, times are changing. We are maturing, perhaps too quickly. Our technology outpaces the wisdom to utilize it. Vast unrest spreads over the globe, and the threat of war looms over most of the more than six billion persons alive today.

Wicca as a religion is changing too. This is necessary if it is to be more than a curiosity of an earlier age. The heirs of Wicca must point their religion firmly to the future if it is to have something to offer coming generations.

Since we have arrived at the point where one mishap could end our planet as we know it, there has never been a time when Wicca as a nature-reverencing religion has had more to offer.

This book breaks many Wicca conventions. It has been structured so that anyone, anywhere in the world, can practice Wicca. No initiations are required. It is designed for the solitary practitioner, since finding others with similar interests is difficult, especially in rural areas.

Wicca is a joyous religion springing from our kinship with nature. It is a merging with the goddesses and gods, the universal energies that created all in existence. It is a personal, positive celebration of life.

And now it is available to all.

Section I
Theory

Wicca and Shamanism

SHAMANISM HAS BEEN defined as the first religion. It existed prior to the earliest civilizations, before our ancestors took the first steps down the long journey to the present. Prior to this time, the shamans were the medicine people, the power wielders, male and female. They wrought magic and spoke to the spirits of nature.

The shamans were the first humans with knowledge. They created, discovered, nurtured, and used it. Knowledge is power; women and men who possessed it in those far-flung days were shamans.

How did shamans capture or discover this power? Through ecstasy—alternate states of consciousness in which they communed with the forces of the universe. Early shamans first attained this state through the use of such "tools" as fasts, thirsts, self-infliction of pain, ingestion of hallucinogenic substances, concentration, and so on. Once mastered, these techniques allowed them to gain awareness of other, nonphysical worlds.

Through such "awareness shifts," all magical knowledge was obtained. Conference with spirits and deities, plants and animals opened up new vistas of learning. Among their own people, the shamans often shared some of this knowledge but reserved the rest for personal use. Shamanic lore wasn't for public consumption.

Later, shamans advanced in the use of tools to facilitate these awareness shifts, marking the advent of magical ritual. Shamans around the world still use tools such as drums, rattles, reflective objects, music, chants, and dance. Indeed, the most effective shamanic rites are those that utilize both natural and artificial tools—a sighing wind, roaring ocean, flickering firelight, steady drumbeat, hiss of rattle. These, combined with darkness and chants, eventually overwhelm the senses, forcing a shifting from awareness of the physical world to the vaster realm of energies. Such are shamanic rites that exist to this day.

From these primitive beginnings arose all magic and religion, including Wicca. Despite current controversy as to the "antiquity" of Wicca, it is spiritually descended from such rites. Though refined and changed for our world, Wicca still touches our souls and causes ecstasy—awareness shifts—uniting us with deity. Many of the techniques of Wicca are shamanic in origin.

Wicca, therefore, can be described as a shamanic religion. As with shamanism, only a select few feel compelled to enter its circle of light.

Today, Wicca has dropped the ordeals of pain and the use of hallucinogens in favor of chanting, meditation, concentration, visualization, music, dance, invocation, and ritual drama. With these spiritual tools, the Wicca achieve a state of ritual consciousness similar to those attained by the most brutal shamanic ordeals.

I deliberately used the term "alternate states of consciousness." Such changed consciousness states aren't unnatural, but are a deviation from the "normal" waking consciousness. Wicca teaches that nature includes a broad spectrum of mental and spiritual states of which most of us are ignorant. Effective Wiccan ritual enables us to slip into such states, allowing communication and communion with the Goddess and God.

Unlike some religions, Wicca doesn't view deity as distant. The Goddess and God are both within ourselves and manifest in all nature. This is the universality: there is nothing that isn't of the gods.

A study of shamanism reveals much of the heart of magical and religious experience in general, and Wicca in particular (see bibliography for recommended books). With ritual as a means to enter ritual consciousness, the shaman or Wicca constantly expands his or her knowledge, and knowledge is power. Wicca helps its practitioners to understand the universe and our place within it.

At present, Wicca is a religion with many variations. Because it is such a personally structured system, I can only state generalities about its creed and form here, filtered through my experience and knowledge, to create a picture of the nature of Wicca.

Wicca, in common with many other religions, recognizes deity as dual. It reveres both the Goddess and the God. They are equal, warm, and loving, not distant or resident in "heaven," but omnipresent throughout the universe.

Wicca also teaches that the physical world is one of many realities. The physical is not the absolute highest expression, nor is the spiritual "purer" than the base. The only difference between the physical and the spiritual is that the former is denser.

As in eastern religions, Wicca also embraces the doctrine of reincarnation, that much-misunderstood subject. Unlike some eastern philosophies, however, Wicca doesn't teach that upon physical death our souls will reincarnate in anything other than a human body. Also, few of the Wicca believes we began our existence as rocks, trees, snails, or birds before we evolved to the point where we could incarnate as human beings. Though these creatures and substances do possess a type of soul, it's not the sort we humans have.

Reincarnation is accepted as fact by many millions in the east and west. It answers many questions: what happens after death? Why do we seem to remember things we've never done in this life? Why are we sometimes strangely attracted to places or people who we've never before seen?

Surely, reincarnation can't answer all these questions, but it is there for those who wish to study it. This isn't something that should be believed. Through contemplation, meditation, and self-analysis, many come to the point where they accept reincarnation as fact. For more information on this subject see chapter 10, "The Spiral of Rebirth."

The Wiccan ideal of morality is simple: do what you want, as long as you harm none. This rule contains another unwritten condition: do nothing that will harm yourself. Thus, if you as a Wicca abuse your body, deny it the necessities of life, or otherwise harm yourself, you're in violation of this principle.

This is more than survival. It also ensures that you'll be in good condition to take on the tasks of preserving and bettering our world, for concern and love for our planet play major roles in Wicca.

Wicca is a religion that utilizes magic. This is one of its most appealing and unique features. Religious magic? This isn't as strange as it might seem. Catholic priests use "magic" to transform a piece of bread into the body of a long-deceased "savior." Prayer—a common tool in many religions—is simply a form of concentration and communication with deity. If the concentration is extended, energies are sent out with the thoughts that may in time make the prayer come true. Prayer is a form of religious magic.

Magic is the practice of moving natural (though little-understood) energies to effect needed change. In Wicca, magic is used as a tool to sanctify ritual areas, and to improve ourselves and the world in which we live.

Many people confuse Wicca and magic as if the two words were interchangeable. Wicca is a religion that embraces magic. If you seek only to practice magic, Wicca probably isn't the answer for you.

Another fundamental point: magic isn't a means of forcing nature to do your will. This is a completely erroneous idea, fostered by the belief that magic is somehow supernatural, as if anything that exists can be outside of nature. *Magic is natural.* It is a harmonious movement of energies to create needed change. If you wish to practice magic, all thoughts of it being paranormal or supernatural must be forgotten.

Most Wiccans don't believe in predestination. Although we honor and revere the Goddess and God, we know that we're free souls with full control and responsibility of our lives. We can't point at an image of an evil god, such as Satan, and blame it for our faults and weaknesses. We can't blame fate. Every second of each day we're creating our futures, shaping the courses of our lives. Once a Wiccan takes full responsibility for all that she or he has done (in this life and past ones) and determines that future actions will be in accord with higher ideals and goals, magic will blossom and life will be a joy.

That perhaps is at the core of Wicca—it is a joyous union with nature. The earth is a manifestation of divine energy. Wicca's temples are flower-splashed meadows, forests, beaches, and deserts. When a Wicca is outdoors, she or he is actually surrounded by sanctity, much as is a Christian when entering a church or cathedral.

Additionally, all nature is constantly singing to us, revealing her secrets. Wiccans listen to the earth. They don't shut out the lessons that she is so desperately trying to teach us. When we lose touch with our blessed planet, we lose touch with deity.

These are some of the basic principles of Wicca. They are the true Wicca; the rituals and myths are secondary to these ideals and serve to celebrate them.

The Standing Stones Book of Shadows (ritual book) included in section III is a guide to constructing your own ritual. Because these rituals are outer form only, you needn't be chained to them. Change rites as the mood strikes you. As long as the rite attunes you with the deities, all is fine.

Don't shut out the physical world in favor of the spiritual or magical realms, for only through nature can we experience these realities. We are here on the earth for a reason. Do, however, use ritual to expand your awareness so that you are truly at one with all creation.

The way is open. The ancient Goddess and God await within and around you. May they bless you with wisdom and power.

2

The Deities

ALL RELIGIONS ARE structures built upon reverence of deity. Wicca is no exception. The Wicca acknowledge a supreme divine power, unknowable, ultimate, from which the entire universe sprang.

The concept of this power, far beyond our comprehension, has nearly been lost in Wicca because of our difficulty in relating to it. Wiccans, however, link with this force through their deities. In accordance with the principles of nature, the supreme power was personified into two basic beings: the Goddess and the God.

Every deity that has received worship upon this planet exists with the archetypal God and Goddess. The complex pantheons of deities that arose in many parts of the world are simply aspects of the two. Every goddess is resident within the concept of the Goddess; every god in the God.

Wicca reveres these twin deities because of its links with nature. Since most (but certainly not all) nature is divided into gender, the deities embodying it are similarly conceived.

In the past, when the Goddess and God were as real as the moon and sun, rites of worship and adoration were unstructured—spontaneous, joyous union with the divine. Later, rituals followed the course of the sun through its astronomical year (and thusly the seasons) as well as the monthly waxing and waning of the moon.

Today similar rites are observed by the Wicca, and their regular performance creates a truly magical closeness with these deities and the powers behind them.

Fortunately, we needn't wait for ritual occasions to be reminded of the Gods' presence. The sight of a perfect blossom in a field of bare earth can instill feelings rivaling those of the most powerful formal rite. Living in nature makes every moment a ritual. Wiccans are comfortable in communicating with animals, plants and trees. They feel energies within stones and sand, and cause fossils to speak of their primeval beginnings. For some Wiccans, watching the sun or moon rise and set each day is a ritual unto itself, for these are the heavenly symbols of the God and Goddess.

Because the Wicca see deity inherent in nature, many of us are involved in ecology—saving the earth from utter destruction by our own hands. The Goddess and God still exist, as they have always existed, and to honor them we honor and preserve our precious planet.

In Wiccan thought, the deities didn't exist before our spiritual ancestor's acknowledgement of them. However, the *energies* behind them did; they created us. Early worshippers recognized these forces as the Goddess and God, personifying them in an attempt to understand them.

The Old Ones didn't die when the ancient pagan religions fell to Christianity in Europe. Most of the rites vanished, but they weren't the only effective ones. Wicca is alive and well and the deities respond to our calls and invocations.

When envisioning the Goddess and God, many of the Wicca see them as well-known deities from ancient religions. Diana, Pan, Isis, Hermes, Hina, Tammuz, Hecate, Ishtar, Cerridwen, Thoth, Tara, Aradia, Artemis, Pélé, Apollo, Kanaloa, Bridget, Helios, Bran, Lugh, Hera, Cybele, Inanna, Maui, Ea, Athena, Lono, Marduk—the list is virtually endless. Many of these deities, with their corresponding histories, rites, and mythic information, furnish the concept of deity for Wiccans.

Some feel comfortable associating such names and forms with the Goddess and God, feeling that they can't possibly revere nameless divine beings. Others find a lack of names and costumes a comforting lack of limitations.

As stated earlier, the Wicca as outlined in this book is "new," although built upon established rituals and myths, firmly rooted within the earliest religious feelings that nature aroused within our species. In these rituals I've used the words "the God" and "the Goddess" rather than specific names such as Diana and Pan. Anyone with a special affinity with particular deities should feel free to adapt the rituals in section III: *The Standing Stones Book of Shadows* to include them.

If you haven't studied non-western polytheistic religions or developed a rapport with divinities other than those with which you were raised, start by accepting this premise (if only for the moment): deity is twin, consisting of the Goddess and the God.

They have been given so many names they have been called the Nameless Ones. In appearance they look exactly as we wish them to, for they're all the deities that ever were. The Goddess and God are all-powerful because they are the creators of all manifest and unmanifest existence. We can contact and communicate with them because a part of us is in them and they are within us.

The Goddess and God are equal; neither is higher or more deserving of respect. Though some Wiccans focus their rituals toward the Goddess and seem to forget the God entirely, this is a reaction to centuries of stifling patriarchal religion, and the loss of acknowledgement of the feminine aspect of divinity. Religion based entirely on feminine energy, however, is as unbalanced and unnatural as one totally masculine in focus. The ideal is a perfect balance of the two. The Goddess and God are equal, complementary.

The Goddess

The Goddess is the universal mother. She is the source of fertility, endless wisdom, and loving caresses. As the Wicca know her, she is often of three aspects: the maiden, the mother, and the crone, symbolized in the waxing, full, and waning moon. She is at once the unploughed field, the full harvest, and the dormant, frost-covered earth. She gives birth to abundance. But as life is her gift, she lends it with the promise of death. This is not darkness and oblivion, but rest from the toils of physical existence. It is human existence between incarnations.

Since the Goddess is nature, all nature, she is both the temptress and the crone; the tornado and the fresh spring rain; the cradle and the grave.

But though she is possessed of both natures, the Wicca revere her as the giver of fertility, love, and abundance, though they acknowledge her darker side as well. We see her in the moon, the soundless, ever-moving sea, and in the green growth of the first spring. She is the embodiment of fertility and love.

The Goddess has been known as the Queen of Heaven, Mother of the Gods that Made the Gods, the Divine Source, the Universal Matrix, the Great Mother, and by countless other titles.

Many symbols are used in Wicca to honor her, such as the cauldron, cup, labrys, five-petaled flowers, the mirror, necklace, seashell, pearl, silver, emerald . . . to name a few.

As she has dominion over the earth, sea and moon, her creatures are varied and numerous. A few include the rabbit, the bear, the owl, the cat, dog, bat, goose, cow, dolphin, lion, horse, wren, scorpion, spider, and bee. All are sacred to the Goddess.

The Goddess has been depicted as a huntress running with her hounds; a celestial deity striding across the sky with stardust falling from her heels; the eternal Mother heavy with child; the weaver of our lives and deaths; a crone walking by waning moonlight seeking out the weak and forlorn, and as many other beings. But no matter how we envision her, she is omnipresent, changeless, eternal.

The God

The God has been revered for eons. He is neither the stern, all-powerful deity of Christianity and Judaism, nor is he simply the consort of the Goddess. God or Goddess, they are equal, one.

We see the God in the sun, brilliantly shining overhead during the day, rising and setting in the endless cycle that governs our lives. Without the sun we could not exist; therefore it has been revered as the source of all life, the warmth that bursts the dormant seeds into life and hastens the greening of the earth after the cold snows of winter.

The God is also tender of the wild animals. As the horned God he is sometimes seen wearing horns on his head, symbolizing his connection with these beasts. In earlier times, hunting was one of the activities thought to be ruled by the God, while the domestication of animals was seen to be Goddess-oriented.

The God's domains include forests untouched by human hands, burning deserts, and towering mountains. The stars, since they are but distant suns, are sometimes thought to be under his domain.

The yearly cycle of greening, maturation, and harvest has long been associated with the sun, hence the solar festivals of Europe (further discussed in chapter 8, "The Days of Power") that are still observed in Wicca.

The God is the fully ripened harvest, intoxicating wine pressed from grapes, golden grain waving in a lone field, shimmering apples hanging from verdant boughs on October afternoons.

With the Goddess, he also celebrates and rules sex. The Wicca don't avoid sex or speak of it in hushed words. It's a part of nature and is accepted as such. Since it brings pleasure, shifts our awareness away from the everyday world, and perpetuates our species, it is thought to be sacred. The God lustily imbues us with the urge that ensures our species' biological future.

Symbols often used to depict or to worship the God include the sword, horns, spear, candle, gold, brass, diamond, sickle, arrow, magical wand, trident, knife, and others. Creatures sacred to him include the bull, dog, snake, fish, stag, dragon, wolf, boar, eagle, falcon, shark, lizard, and many others.

Of old, the God was the Sky Father, and the Goddess, the Earth Mother. The God of the sky, of rain and lightning, descended upon and united with the Goddess, spreading seed upon the land, celebrating her fertility.

Today the deities of Wicca are still firmly associated with fertility, but every aspect of human existence can be linked with the Goddess and God. They can be called upon to help us sort through the vicissitudes of our existences and bring joy into our often spiritually bereft lives.

This doesn't mean that when problems occur we should leave them in the hands of the Goddess. This is a stalling maneuver, an avoidance of dealing with the bumps on the road of life. As Wiccans, however, we can call on the Goddess and God to clear our minds and to *help us help ourselves*. Magic is an excellent means of accomplishing this. After attuning with the Goddess and God, Wiccans ask their assistance during the magical rite that usually follows.

Beyond this, the Goddess and God can help us change our lives. Because the deities *are* the creative forces of the universe (not just symbols), we can call upon them to empower our rites and to bless our magic. Again, this is in direct opposition to most religions. The power is in the hands of every practitioner, not specialized priests or priestesses who perform these feats for the masses. This is what makes Wicca a truly satisfying way of life. We have direct links with the deities. No intermediaries are needed; no priests or confessors or shamans. *We are the shamans.*

To develop a rapport with the Goddess and God, a necessity for those who desire to practice Wicca, you might wish to follow these simple rituals.

At night, stand or sit facing the moon, if it is visible. If not, imagine the fullest moon you've ever seen glowing silver-white in the inky blackness, directly above and before you.

Feel the soft lunar light streaming onto your skin. Sense it touching and mixing with your own energies, commingling and forming new patterns.

See the Goddess in any form that you will. Call to her, chanting old names if you wish: Diana, Lucina, Selena (pronouncing them as: Dee-AH-nah, Loo-CHEE-nah, Say-LEE-nah). Open your heart and mind to the aspect of Goddess-energy manifested in the moon's light.

Repeat this daily for one week, preferably at the same time each night.

Concurrently with this exercise, attune with the God. Upon rising in the morning, no matter how late it is, stand before the sun (through a window if necessary; outside if possible) and soak in its energies. Think about the God. Visualize him as you wish. It might be as a mighty warrior rippling with muscles, a spear upraised in one hand, the other cradling a child or a bunch of dew-dripping grapes.

You may want to chant God names, such as Kernunnos, Osiris, Apollo (Care-NOON-nos, Oh-SIGH-ris, Ah-PALL-low) as with the Goddess.

If you don't wish to visualize the God (for visualization can impose limitations), simply attune to the energies pouring down from the sun. Even if clouds fill the sky, the God's energies will still reach you. Feel them with all your magical imagination (See chapter 11, "Exercises and Magical Techniques").

Let no thoughts but those of the God disturb your revery. Reach out with your feelings; open your awareness to higher things. Call upon the God in any words. Express your desire to attune with him.

Practice these exercises daily for one week. If you wish to explore the concepts of the Goddess and God, read books on mythology from any country in the world. Read the myths but look for their underlying themes. The more you read, the more information you'll have at your fingertips; eventually it will merge into a nonstructured but extremely complex knowledge bank concerning the deities. In other words, you'll begin to know them.

If, after seven days, you feel the need (or the desire), continue these exercises until you feel comfortable with the Goddess and God. They've been in us and around us all the time; we need only open ourselves to this awareness. This is one of the secrets of Wicca—deity dwells within.

In your quest to know the gods, take long walks beneath trees. Study flowers and plants. Visit wild, natural places and feel the energies of the Goddess and God directly—through the rush of a stream, the pulse of energy from an old oak's trunk, the heat of a sun-warmed rock. Familiarizing yourself with the existence of the deities comes more easily through actual contact with such power sources.

Next, when you've achieved this state, you may wish to set up a temporary or permanent shrine or altar to the Goddess and God. This needn't be more than a small table, two candles, an incense burner, and a plate or bowl to hold offerings of flowers, fruit, grain, seed, wine, or milk. Place the two candles in their holders to the rear of the shrine.

The candle on the left represents the Goddess; that on the right the God. Colors are often used to distinguish between the two; a red candle for the God and a green one to honor the Goddess. This ties in with the nature-associations of Wicca, for green and red are ancient magical colors linked with life and death. Other colors can be used—yellow or gold to honor the God, and white or silver for the Goddess.

Before and between these candles place the incense burner, and in front of this the plate or offering bowl. A vase of seasonal flowers can also be added, as can any personal power objects such as crystals, fossils, and dried herbs.

To begin a simple ritual to the Gods at your shrine, stand before it with an offering of some kind in your hand. Light the candles and incense, place the offering in the bowl or plate, and say such words as these:

Lady of the moon, of the restless sea and verdant earth,
lord of the sun and of the wild creatures,
accept this offering I place here in your honor.
Grant me the wisdom to see your presence in all nature,
O Great Ones!

Goddess candle	Flowers	God candle
	Censer	
	Offering plate	

Layout of the shrine

Afterward, sit or stand for a few minutes in contemplation of the deities and of your growing relationship with them. Feel them inside and around you. Then quench the flames (use your fingers, a candle snuffer, or a knife blade. Blowing them out is an affront to the element* of fire). Allow the incense to burn itself out, and continue on with your day or night.

If you wish, go before the shrine once a day at a prescribed time. This may be upon rising, just before sleep, or after lunch. Light the candles, attune and commune with the Goddess and God. This isn't necessary, but the steady rhythm set up by this cycle is beneficial and will improve your relationship with the deities.

Return the offerings left on the shrine to the earth at the end of each day, or when you bring more to leave.

If you cannot erect a permanent shrine, set it up each time you feel the need to use it, then store the articles away. Make the placing of the objects on the shrine a part of the ritual.

This simple rite belies its powers. The Goddess and God are real, viable entities, possessing the force that created the universe. Attuning with them changes us forever. It also sparks new hope for our planet and for our continued existence upon it.

If this rite is too formalized for you, change it or write your own. This is the basic thrust of this book: do it your way, not my way simply because I've set it down on paper. I can never fit my feet into someone else's footprints on the sand. There's no one true right and only way in Wicca; that thinking belongs to monotheistic religions that have largely become political and business institutions.

Discovering the deities of Wicca is a never-ending experience. They constantly reveal themselves. As the shamans say, "Be attentive." All nature is singing to us of her secrets. The Goddess constantly draws aside her veil; the God lights us up with inspiration and illumination. We simply don't notice.

---

* See glossary.

Don't worry what others might think if they knew you were attuning with a twenty-thousand-year-old Goddess. Their feelings and thoughts concerning your religion are of no consequence. If you feel the need to shelter your experiences from others, do so, not out of fear or embarrassment, but because we're truly all on separate paths. Everyone isn't suited to Wicca.

There are some who say that we (and anyone else who won't follow their rituals or embrace their theology) are worshipping Satan. Not that we know it, of course; Satan is too tricky for that, according to these experts.

Such people can't believe that any religion but their own can be meaningful, fulfilling, and true to its adherent. So if we worship the God and Goddess, they say, we're denying all good and are worshipping Satan, the embodiment of all negativity and evil.

Wiccans aren't so close-minded. Perhaps it's the greatest of all human vanities to assume that one's religion is the only way to deity. Such beliefs have caused incalculable bloodshed and the rise of the hideous concept of holy wars.

The basis of this misconception seems to be the concept of a pristine, pure, positive being—God. If this deity is the sum of all good, worshippers believe that there must be an equally negative one as well. Thus, Satan.

The Wicca don't accept such ideas. *We acknowledge the dark aspects of the Goddess and the God as well as the bright.* All nature is composed of opposites, and this polarity is also resident within ourselves. The darkest human traits as well as the brightest are locked within our unconsciousness. It is only our ability to rise above destructive urges, to channel such energies into positive thoughts and actions, that separates us from mass-murderers and sociopaths.

Yes, the God and Goddess have dark aspects, but this needn't scare us off. Look at some of the manifestations of their powers. From a ravaging flood comes rich soil in which new plants thrive. Death brings a deeper appreciation of life to the living and rest for the transcended one. "Good" and "evil" are often identical in nature, depending on one's viewpoint. Additionally, out of every evil, some good is eventually born.

Any and all religions are real, the genuine article, to their practitioners. There can never be one religion, prophet, or savior that will satisfy all six billion humans. Each of us must find our ideal way to attune with deity. For some, it's Wicca.

Wiccans emphasize the bright aspects of the deities because this gives us purpose to grow and evolve to the highest realm of existence. When death, destruction, hurt, pain, and anger appear in our lives (as they must), we can turn to the Goddess and God and know that this is a part of them too. We needn't blame a devil on these natural aspects of life and call upon a pure-white god to fend them off.

In truly understanding the Goddess and God, one comes to understand life, for the two are inextricably entwined. Live your earthly life fully, but try to see the spiritual aspects of your activities as well. Remember—the physical and spiritual are but reflections of each other.

When I give classes, one question seems to come up frequently:

"What is the meaning of life?"

It may be asked with a laugh, but this is the one question that, if answered, satisfies any others we may have. It is the problem every religion and philosophical system has struggled to solve.

Anyone can find the answer through the simple technique of living and observing life. Though two people won't find the same answers, they can find them together.

The Goddess and God are of nature, both the delightful and the dark. We don't worship nature as such; some Wiccans probably wouldn't even say that they worship the Goddess and God. We don't bow down to the deities; we work with them to create a better world.

This is what makes Wicca a truly participatory religion.

3

Magic

IT'S COMMON KNOWLEDGE even among the masses that Witches practice magic. They may have misguided ideas concerning the type of magic performed, but the Witch is firmly linked in popular thought with the magical arts.

Wicca is, as we have seen, a religion that embraces magic as one of its basic concepts. This isn't unusual. In fact, it's often difficult to discern where religion ends and magic begins in any faith.

Still, magic plays a special role in Wicca. It allows us to improve our lives and return energy to our ravaged planet. Wiccans also develop special relationships with the Goddess and God through magic. This doesn't mean that every spell is a prayer, nor are invocations differently worded spells. Through working with the powers that the God and the Goddess embody, we grow close to them. Calling upon their names and visualizing their presence during spells and rites creates a bond between deity and human. Thus, in Wicca, magic is a religious practice.

I've defined magic a number of times in my books. Surprisingly, this is a difficult task. My latest, most refined definition is:

Magic is the projection of natural energies to produce needed effects.

There are three main sources of this energy—personal power, earth power, and divine power.

Personal power is the life force that sustains our earthly existences. It powers our bodies. We absorb energy from the moon and sun, from water and food. We release it during movement, exercise, sex, and childbirth. Even exhaling releases some power, though we recoup the loss through inhaling.

In magic, personal power is aroused, infused with a specific purpose, released, and directed toward its goal.

Earth power is that which resides within our planet and in its natural products. Stones, trees, wind, flames, water, crystals, and scents all possess unique, specific powers that can be used during magical ritual.

A Wiccan may dip a quartz crystal in salt water to cleanse it and then press it against an ailing person's body to send its healing energies within. Or, herbs may be sprinkled around a candle that is burned to produce a specific magical effect. Oils are rubbed onto the body to effect internal changes.

Divine power is the manifestation of personal power and earth power. This is the energy that exists within the Goddess and God—the life force, the source of universal power that created everything in existence.

Wiccans invoke the Goddess and God to bless their magic with power. During ritual they may direct personal power to the deities, asking that a specific need be met. This is truly religious magic.

And so, magic is a process in which Wiccans work in harmony with the universal power source that we envision as the Goddess and God, as well as with personal and earth energies, to improve our lives and to lend energy to Earth. Magic is a method whereby individuals under none but self-determined predestination take control of their lives.

Contrary to popular belief, magic isn't supernatural. True, it is an occult (hidden) practice steeped in millennia of secrecy, slander, and misinformation, but it is a natural practice utilizing genuine powers that haven't yet been discovered or labeled by science.

This doesn't invalidate magic. Even scientists don't claim to know everything about our universe. If they did, the field of scientific investigation wouldn't exist. The powers the Wiccans use will eventually be documented and so lose their mystery. Such has already partially occurred with hypnotism and psychology, and may soon happen to extrasensory perception. Magnetism, indeed, was a firmly established aspect of magic until it was "discovered" by science. But even today, magnets are used in spells and charms, and such forces as these call up strange, old feelings.

Play with two magnets. See the invisible forces resisting and attracting in seemingly supernatural ways.

Magic is similar. Though it appears to be completely nonsensical, with no basis in fact, it operates along its own rules and logic. Simply because it isn't fully understood doesn't mean that it doesn't exist. Magic is effective in causing manifestations of needed change.

This isn't self-deception. Correctly performed magic works, and no amount of explaining away alters this fact.

Here's a description of a typical candle ritual. I'll use myself as an example. Say I need to pay a hundred-dollar phone bill but don't have the money. My magical goal: the means to pay the bill.

I decide to use a ritual to help focus my concentration and visualization (See chapter 11, "Exercises and Magical Techniques"). Checking my magical supplies, I discover that I have green candles, patchouli oil, a good selection of money-drawing herbs, parchment paper, and green ink.

At my altar, I light the candles representing the Goddess and the God while silently invoking their presence. Next, I ignite a charcoal block and sprinkle cinnamon and sage onto the block as a magical prosperity incense.

I draw a picture of the phone bill on the paper, clearly marking the amount in numerals. While drawing, I visualize that the paper is no longer just a piece of paper; it is the bill itself.

Then I sketch a square around the bill, symbolizing my control over it, and mark a large "x" through it, effectively canceling out its existence (as will occur when it is paid).

I now start to visualize the bill being paid in full. I might write this over the picture, making it appear to have been stamped with these words. I visualize myself looking in my checkbook, seeing that the balance will cover the check, and then writing the check itself.

Next, I rub a green candle with patchouli oil, from each end to the middle, while saying something like the following:

I call upon the powers of the Mother Goddess and the Father God;
I call upon the forces of the earth, air, fire and water;
I call upon the sun, moon and stars
to bring me the funds to pay this bill.

Still visualizing, I place the candle in the holder directly over the picture of the bill. I sprinkle herbs around the candle's base, stating (and visualizing) that each is lending its energy toward my goal:

Sage, herb of Jupiter, send your powers to my spell.
Cinnamon, herb of the sun, send your powers to my spell.

Once this is done, still visualizing my bill as paid in full, I light the candle and, as its flame shines, release the energy I've built up into the picture.

I let the candle burn for ten, fifteen minutes, or longer, depending on my ability to retain the visualization. I see the candle absorbing the energy I've put into the picture. I see the herbs streaming their energies into the candle flame, and the combined energies of the herbs, candle, patchouli oil, and picture—coupled with my personal power—pouring from the flame and out to bring my magical goal toward manifestation.

When I can do no more, I remove the picture, light it in the candle, hold it as it burns for a few seconds, and then throw it into the small cauldron that sits beside my altar.

Finished, I allow the candle to burn itself out, knowing that the ritual will take effect.

Within a day or two, perhaps a week, I'll either receive unexpected (or delayed) money, or will satisfy other financial obligations in a manner that frees me to pay the bill.

How does it work? From the time I decide to do an act of magic, I'm doing it. Thinking about it sets personal power into motion. Throughout the whole process—gathering supplies, drawing the bill, lighting the candle, visualizing—I'm rousing and infusing personal power with my magical need. During the rite itself, I release this power into the candle. When I finally burn the picture, the last of these energies are released and free, set to work to arrange for me to pay the bill.

I may not be able to tell you exactly *how* magic works, only that it does work. Fortunately, we don't have to know this; all we must know is how to make it work.

I'm no expert in electricity, but I can plug my toaster into a wall socket and burn my whole wheat bread. Similarly, in magic we "plug into" energies that stretch, crisscross, and zip around and through us.

There are many ways to practice magic. Wiccans generally choose simple, natural forms, though some enjoy heavy ceremony, borrowing from the classical grimoires such as *The Key of Solomon* (see bibliography). Usually, however, practicing magic involves herbs, crystals, and rocks; the use of symbols and color; magical gestures, music, voice, dance, and trance; astral projection, meditation, concentration, and visualization.

There are literally thousands of magical systems, even in Wicca. For instance, numerous magical ways exist to use crystals, or herbs, or symbols, and by combining them more systems are created.

Many, many books have been published outlining magical systems, and some of these are listed in the bibliography. In my books I've discussed the powers of the elements, crystals, and herbs. In this work, the subject of rune magic is explored as an example of a self-contained magical system with hints at combining it with others.

Such systems aren't necessary to the successful practice of magic. Performing magical rituals simply by manipulating tools such as herbs and crystals will be ineffective, for the true power of magic lies within ourselves—the gift of deity.

So no matter the magical system, personal power must be infused with the need and then released. In Wiccan magic, personal power is recognized as our direct link with the Goddess and God. Magic, therefore, is a religious act in which Wiccans unite with their deities to better themselves and their world.

This is important—magic is a positive practice. *Wiccans don't perform destructive, manipulative, or exploitive magic.* Because they recognize that the power at work in magic is, ultimately, derived from the Goddess and God, negative workings are absolutely taboo. "Evil" magic is an insult to themselves, to the human race, to Earth, the

Goddess and God, and the universe itself. The repercussions can be imagined. The energies of magic are those of life itself.

Anyone can practice magic—within a religious context or not. If certain words or gestures pop into your mind while performing a spell, and they seem right, by all means use them. If you can't find a ritual to your liking or that fits your needs, create one. You needn't write fancy poetry or choreography for thirty singing incense bearers and thirteen singing priestesses.

If nothing else, light a candle, settle down before it, and concentrate on your magical need. Trust yourself.

If you truly desire to know the nature of magic, practice it! Many are afraid of magic. They've been taught (by nonpractitioners) that it's dangerous. Don't be scared. Crossing the street is dangerous too. But if you do it properly, you're fine.

Of course, the only way you'll find this out is to cross that street. If your magic is infused with love, you'll be in no danger whatsoever.

Call upon the Goddess and God to protect you and teach you the secrets of magic. Ask stones and plants to reveal their powers—and listen. Read as much as you can, discarding negative or disturbing information.

Learn by doing, and the Goddess and God will bless you with all that you truly need.

4

Tools

IN COMMON WITH most religions, certain objects are used in Wicca for ritual purposes. These tools invoke the deities, banish negativity, and direct energy through our touch and intention.

Some of the tools of the Witch (the broom, cauldron, and magic wand) have gained firm places in contemporary folklore and myth. Through the popularization of folktales and the work of Disney studios, millions know that cauldrons are used to brew up potions and that wands transform the drab into the beautiful. Most folks, however, don't know the powerful magic behind such tools and their inner symbolism within Wicca.

To practice Wicca, you may want to collect at least some of these tools. Search through antique and junk shops, swap meets, and flea markets for these treasures. Or, write or email occult suppliers (addresses in appendix I). Though difficult to find, your ritual tools are well worth any efforts expended to obtain them.

These tools aren't necessary to the practice of Wicca. They do, however, enrich rituals and symbolize complex energies. The tools have no power save for that which we lend to them.

Some say that we should use magical tools until we no longer need them. Perhaps it's better to use them as long as you feel comfortable in doing so.

The Broom

Witches use brooms in magic and ritual. It is a tool sacred to both the Goddess and God. This is nothing new; pre-Colombian Mexico saw the worship of a type of Witch deity, Tlazelteotl, who was pictured riding naked on a broom. The Chinese worship a broom goddess who is invoked to bring clear weather in times of rain.

Then too, probably because of its phallic shape, the broom became a powerful tool against curses and practitioners of evil magic. Laid across the threshold, the broom halted all spells sent to the house or those resident within. A broom under the pillow brought pleasant dreams and guarded the sleeper.

European Witches became identified with the broom because both were infused with magic in religious and popular thought. Witches were accused of flying on broomsticks, and this was considered proof of their alliance with "dark powers." Such an act, if it could be performed, would indeed be supernatural and, therefore, of the Devil in their eyes, in contrast to the simple healing and love spells that Witches actually performed. Of course, the tale was invented by Witch persecutors.*

Today the broom is still used in Wicca. A Wicca may begin a ritual by sweeping the area (indoors or out) lightly with the magic broom. After this, the altar is set up, the tools carried out, and the ritual is ready to begin (See chapter 13, "Ritual Design").

This sweeping is more than a physical cleansing. In fact, the broom's bristles needn't touch the ground. While brushing, the Wiccan visualizes the broom sweeping out the astral buildup that occurs where humans live. This purifies the area to allow smoother ritual workings.

Since it is a purifier, the broom is linked with the element of water. Thus it is also used in all types of water spells, including those of love and psychic workings.

Many Witches collect brooms, and indeed their endless variety and the exotic materials used in their manufacture make this an interesting hobby.

---

* Some Wiccans claim that brooms were "ridden" while hopping along the ground, much as are hobby-horses, to promote fertility of the fields. Then, too, it is believed that tales of Witches riding brooms through the air were unsophisticated explanations of astral projection.

If you wish to make your magic broom, you might try the old magical formula of an ash staff, birch twigs, and a willow binding. The ash is protective, the birch is purifying, and the willow is sacred to the Goddesss.

Of course, a branch from any tree or bush can be used in place of the broom (while cutting it, thank the tree for its sacrifice, using such words as will be found in the "An Herbal Grimoire" section of *The Standing Stones Book of Shadows,* section III). A tiny broom of pine needles can also be used.

In early American slave weddings, as well as Gypsy nuptials, the couple often ritually jumped a broomstick to solemnize their union. Such marriages were quite common until recent times, and even today Wiccan and pagan handfastings often include a broom leap.

There are many old spells involving brooms. In general, the broom is a purificatory and protective instrument, used to ritually cleanse the area for magic or to guard a home by laying it across the threshold, under the bed, in windowsills, or on doors.

The broom used for magic, as with all magical tools, should be reserved for this purpose only. If you decide to buy a broom, try to find a round one; the flat Shaker-type brooms just don't seem to have the same effect.*

Wand

The wand is one of the prime magical tools. It has been used for thousands of years in magical and religious rites. It is an instrument of invocation. The Goddess and God may be called to watch the ritual with words and an uplifted wand. It is also sometimes used to direct energy, to draw magical symbols or a circle on the ground, to point toward danger while perfectly balanced on the Witch's palm or arm, or even to stir brew in a cauldron. The wand represents the element of air to some Wiccans, and is sacred to the God.

---

* More broom lore can be found in chapter 13 of *The Magical Household* (Llewellyn, 1987).

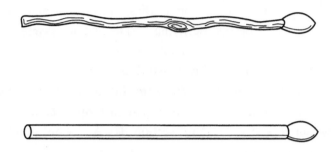

There are traditional woods used for the wand, including willow, elder, oak, apple, peach, hazel, cherry, and so on. Some Wiccans cut it the length from the crook of the elbow to the tip of the forefinger, but this isn't necessary. Any fairly straight piece of wood can be used; even dowels purchased from hardware stores work well, and I've seen beautifully carved and painted wands made from these.

New Age consciousness (and merchandising) has brought the wand into renewed prominence. Delightful, beautiful creations fashioned of silver and quartz crystals are now available in a wide range of sizes and prices. These certainly could be used within Wiccan ritual, though wooden wands have a longer history.

Don't worry about finding the ideal wand at first; one will come to you. I used a length of licorice root as a wand for a while and had good results with it.

Any stick you use will be infused with energy and power. Find one that feels comfortable, and it'll do just fine.

Censer

The censer is an incense burner. It can be a complex, swinging, metal censer like those used in the Catholic church, or a simple seashell. The censer holds the smoldering incense during Wiccan rites.

If you cannot find a suitable censer, make one. Any bowl or cup half-filled with sand or salt will serve well. The salt or sand absorbs the heat from the charcoal or incense and prevents the bowl from cracking.

Incense sticks can also be pushed into the salt, or cones placed upon its surface.

Incense use in ritual and magic is an art in and of itself. When no specific incense is called for in rituals and spells, use your own intuition and creativity in determining which blend to use.

Stick, cone, or block incense can be used, but most Wiccans favor the raw or granulated incense, the type that must be burned on self-igniting charcoal briquettes, available from occult suppliers. Either is fine.

In ceremonial magic, "spirits" are sometimes commanded to appear in visible form in the smoke rising from the censer. While this isn't part of Wicca, the Goddess and God can sometimes be seen in the curling, twisting smoke. Sitting while breathing slowly and watching the smoke can be an entrancing act, and you might slip into an alternate state of consciousness.

Wiccan ritual, when performed indoors, isn't complete without incense. Outdoors a fire often substitutes, or stick-type incense is stuck into the ground. Thus, the censer is an important tool for indoor rites. To some of the Wicca, the censer represents the element of air. It is often placed before the images of the deities on the altar, if there are any.

Cauldron

The cauldron is the Witch's tool *par excellence.* It is an ancient vessel of cooking and brew making, steeped in magical tradition and mystery. The cauldron is the container in which magical transformations occur; the sacred grail, the holy spring, the sea of primeval creation.

The Wicca see the cauldron as a symbol of the Goddess, the manifested essence of femininity and fertility. It is also symbolic of the element of water, reincarnation, immortality, and inspiration. Celtic legends concerning Kerridwen's cauldron have had a strong impact on contemporary Wicca.

The cauldron is often a focal point of ritual. During spring rites it is sometimes filled with fresh water and flowers; during winter a fire may be kindled *within* the cauldron to represent the returning heat and light of the sun (the God) from the cauldron (the Goddess). This links in with agricultural myths wherein the God is born in winter, reaches maturity in summer, and dies after the last harvest (see chapter 8, "The Days of Power").

Ideally speaking, the cauldron should be of iron, resting on three legs, with its opening smaller than its widest part. Cauldrons can be difficult to find, even small ones, but a thorough search usually produces some type of cauldron. A few mail-order houses stock cauldrons, but not regularly. You may wish to query these sources.

Cauldrons come in all sizes, ranging from a few inches in diameter to monsters three feet across. I have collected a few, including an old one reserved for ritual purposes.

The cauldron can be an instrument of scrying (gazing) by filling it with water and staring into its inky depths. It can also serve as a container in which to brew up those infamous Wicca brews, but bear in mind that a large fire and plenty of patience are required to make liquids boil in larger cauldrons. Most Wiccans use stoves and cooking pots today.

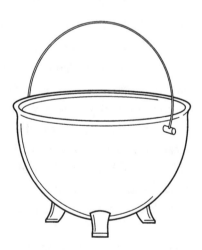

If you have difficulty finding a cauldron, persevere and one will eventually materialize. It certainly can't hurt to ask the Goddess and God to send one your way.

Magic Knife

The magic knife (or athame) has an ancient history. It isn't used for cutting purposes in Wicca, but to direct the energy raised during rites and spells. It is seldom used to invoke or call upon the deities for it is an instrument of commanding and power manipulation. We'd rather invoke the Goddess and God.

The knife is often dull, usually double-edged with a black or dark handle. Black absorbs power. When the knife is used in ritual (see *The Standing Stones Book of Shadows*) to direct energy, some of this power is absorbed into the handle—only a tiny amount—which can be called upon later. Then again, sometimes energy raised within Wiccan ritual is channeled into the knife for later use. The stories of swords with magical powers and names are quite common in mythic literature, and swords are nothing more than large knives.

Some Wiccans engrave their knives with magical symbols, usually taken from *The Key of Solomon,* but this isn't necessary. As with most magical tools, the knife becomes powerful by your touch and usage. If you so desire, however, scratch words, symbols, or runes onto its blade or handle.

A sword is sometimes used in Wicca, as it has all the properties of the knife, but can be difficult for indoor rituals due to its size.

Because of the symbolism of the knife, which is a tool that causes change, it is commonly linked with the element of fire. Its phallic nature links it with the God.

White-Handled Knife

The white-handled knife (sometimes called a *bolline*) is simply a practical, working knife as opposed to the purely ritualistic magic knife. It is used to cut wands or sacred herbs, inscribe symbols onto

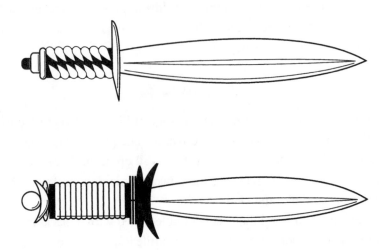

candles or on wood, clay, or wax, and in cutting cords for use in magic. It is usually white-handled to distinguish it from the magic knife.

Some Wiccan traditions dictate that the white-handled knife be used only within the magic circle. This would, of course, limit its usefulness. It seems to me that using it solely for ritual purposes (such as harvesting flowers from the garden to place on the altar during ritual) confirms the tool's sacredness and so allows its use out of "sacred space."

Crystal Sphere

Quartz crystals are extremely popular today, but the quartz crystal sphere is an ancient magical tool. It is exquisitely expensive, selling for twenty dollars to thousands of dollars, depending on size. Most crystal balls on the market today are glass, leaded glass, or even plastic. Genuine quartz crystal spheres can be determined by their high prices and inclusions or irregularities.

The crystal has long been used in contemplative divination. The diviner gazes into the ball until the psychic faculties blossom, and images, seen in the mind or projected by it into the depths of the crystal, reveal the necessary information.

In Wiccan ritual, the crystal is sometimes placed on the altar to represent the Goddess. Its shape (spheroid) is Goddess-symbolic, as are all circles and rounds, and its icy cold temperature (another way to determine genuine rock crystal) is symbolic of the depths of the sea, the Goddess' domain.

Then, too, the crystal may be used to receive messages from the Gods, or to store energy raised in ritual. Some Wiccans scry in the crystal to call up images of the Goddess or of past lives. It is a magical object touched with the divine, and if you find one, guard it carefully.

Periodic exposure to moonlight, or rubbing the crystal with fresh mugwort, will increase its ability to spark our psychic powers. It may be the center of full moon rituals.

Cup

The cup is simply a cauldron on a stem. It symbolizes the Goddess and fertility, and is related to the element of water. Though it can be used to hold water (which is often present on the altar), it may also contain the ritual beverage imbibed during the rite.

The cup can be made of nearly any substance: silver, brass, gold, earthenware, soapstone, alabaster, crystal, and other materials.

Pentacle

The pentacle is usually a flat piece of brass, gold, silver, wood, wax, or clay, inscribed with certain symbols. The most common, and indeed the only necessary one, is the pentagram, the five-pointed star that has been used in magic for millennia.

The pentacle was "borrowed" from ceremonial magic. In this ancient art it was often an instrument of protection, or a tool used to evoke spirits. In Wicca, the pentacle represents the element of earth and is a convenient tool upon which to place amulets, charms, or other objects to be ritually consecrated. It is sometimes used to summon the Gods and Goddesses.

Pentacles are also hung over doors and windows to act as protective devices, or are ritually manipulated to draw money owing to the pentacle's earth associations.

The Book of Shadows

The Book of Shadows is a Wiccan workbook containing invocations, ritual patterns, spells, runes, rules governing magic, and so on. Some Books of Shadows are passed from one Wiccan to another, usually upon initiation, but the vast majority of Books of Shadows today are composed by each individual Wiccan.

Don't believe the stories in most other Wiccan books that one single Book of Shadows has been handed down from antiquity, for each sect of Wicca seems to claim that their own is the original, and they're all different.

Although until recently a Book of Shadows was usually hand-written, today typed or even photocopied versions are quite common. Some Wiccans are even computerizing their books—to create, as friends of mine call it, the "Floppy Disc of Shadows."

To make your own Book of Shadows, begin with any blank book—these are available in most art stores and bookshops. If you cannot find a bound blank book, any lined exercise book will do. Simply write in this book any rituals, spells, invocations, and magical information that you have either composed or found elsewhere and would like to preserve.

Remember—all Books of Shadows (including the one in section III) are suggestions as to ritual, not "holy writ." Never feel tied down to these words. In fact, many Witches use three-ring binders, shuffling around pages, adding or subtracting information from their Book of Shadows at will.

It is a good idea to copy your spells and rites by hand. Not only does this ensure that you've read the work completely, it also allows easier reading by candlelight. Ideally, all rites are memorized (there's nothing more distracting than having to read or glance at the book), or created spontaneously, but if you would read your rites, be sure your copies are legible by flickering firelight.

Bell

The bell is a ritual instrument of incredible antiquity. Ringing a bell unleashes vibrations that have powerful effects according to its volume, tone, and material of construction.

The bell is a feminine symbol and so is often used to invoke the Goddess in ritual. It is also rung to ward off evil spells and spirits, to halt storms, or to evoke good energies. Placed in cupboards or hung on the door, it guards the home. Bells are sometimes rung in ritual to mark various sections and to signal a spell's beginning or end.

Any type of bell can be used.

These are some of the tools used in Wiccan ritual. Working with them, familiarizing yourself with their powers, and pouring your own energy into them, you may find their use becoming second nature. Gathering them is a problem, but this can be seen as a magical test of the seriousness of your Wiccan interest.

As you collect each tool, you can prepare it for ritual. If old, it should be stripped of all associations and energies; you don't know who owned the tool, nor to what purposes it may have been used.

To begin this process, clean the tool physically using the appropriate method. When the object is clean and dry, bury it (in the earth or a bowlful of sand or salt) for a few days, allowing the energies to disperse. An alternate method consists of plunging the tool into the sea, river, or lake, or even your own bathtub after purifying the water by adding a few pinches of salt.

Don't ruin a good piece of wood by wetting it; similarly, don't mar the finish of some other object by allowing it to contact salt. Use the most appropriate method for each tool.

After a few days, dig up the tool, wipe it clean, and it is ready for magic. If you use the water method, leave the object submerged for a few hours, then dry it. If desired, repeat until the tool is clean, refreshed, new.

There are consecration ceremonies for the Wiccan tools in section III, as well as preparation rites in the Herbal Grimoire section there. Both are optional; use as your intuition dictates.

5

Music, Dance, and Gesture

WICCA UNDERSTANDS THAT what we perceive to be the difference between the physical and the nonphysical is due to our limitations as materially based beings. Some of the tools used in the practice of religion are indeed nonphysical. Three of the most effective of these are music, dance, and gesture.*

These techniques are used to raise power, alter consciousness, and to unite with the Goddess and God—to achieve ecstasy. These tools are often part and parcel of ritual, and indeed the most effective, powerful rites can be those exclusively utilizing such tools. (A ritual comprised entirely of gestures can be found in section III: *The Standing Stones Book of Shadows.*)

Music and dance were among the earliest magical and religious acts. Our ancestors probably utilized the magic of hand signals and bodily postures before speech was fully developed. The simple gesture of pointing still has powerful emotional effects, from a witness singling out the defendant as the person involved in the crime, to a hopeful at an audition being selected among a sea of her or his peers.

The first music was probably rhythmic. Humans soon discovered that pleasing rhythms and sounds could be produced by slapping various parts of the body, especially the thighs and chest.

Clapping creates a distinctive, clean sound that is still used by some Wiccans to release personal power during magical ritual.†

---

* Music is, technically speaking, comprised of sound waves that are physically measureable. We can't hold music in our hands, however, merely the instruments that produce it.

† See Doreen Valiente's *Witchcraft For Tomorrow* (New York: St. Martin's Press, 1978), page 182.

Rhythmic instruments such as log drums were later used to produce fuller sounds. Some rocks ring when struck, and so another type of instrument was born. Reeds, bones, and some shells produce whistling sounds when correctly blown. Shamanic systems still in existence use these tools.

Less intellectual rituals can be more effective precisely because they bypass the conscious mind and speak to the deep consciousness, the psychic awareness. Music and dance emotionally involve us in Wiccan rites.

The thought of dancing, singing, or making music embarrasses some of us. This is a natural outgrowth of our increasingly repressive society. In Wicca, however, dance and music occur *before the deities alone*. You aren't performing for a crowd, so don't worry about missing a note or tripping over your feet. *They* don't care, and no one ever need know what you do before the Gods in your rites.

Even the most unmusically inclined can bang two rocks together, shake a rattle, clap hands, or walk in circles. To this day, some of the most established and effective Wiccan covens utilize a simple circular run around the altar to raise power. So much for fancy ritual choreography.

Here's some traditional lore concerning dance, music, and gesture. If you find it appealing, feel free to incorporate it into your Wiccan rituals. But one suggestion: if you find your rites stuffy and unsatisfying, if they don't create a link with the deities, the problem may be a lack of emotional content. Music and dance can produce true involvement in the ritual and so open your awareness of the Goddess and God. During magic they may produce freer access to energy.

Music

Music is simply a re-creation of the sounds of nature. Wind through trees, the roar of the ocean hurling itself against jagged cliffs, pattering rain, the crackling of a lightning-produced fire, the cry of birds, and roars of animals are some of the "instruments" that constitute the music of nature.

Human beings have long integrated music into religious and magical rituals for its powerful effects. Shamans use a steady drum beat to induce trance, and a drum can be used to control the pace of magical dance. Then too, music has long been celebrated for calming ferocious animals—and humans as well.*

Music can be a part of Wiccan workings today. You might simply find appropriate pieces, selected from classical, ethnic, folk, or contemporary sources, and play these during rituals. Musically inclined Wiccans can create music before, during, or after the ritual.

My most satisfying and vivid rituals often involve music. I remember one day I hid a small tape-recorder behind a tree in the Laguna Mountains. Strangely, the music didn't intrude on the setting of wild-flowers, towering pines, and ancient oaks, but heightened my solitary ritual.

If you have proficiency with an instrument, work it into your rituals. A flute, violin, recorder, guitar, folk harp, and other small instruments can easily be introduced into ritual, as can drums, rattles, bells, or even glasses of water and a knife with which to strike them. Other less portable instruments can be recorded and played back during ritual.

Such musical interludes can be used directly *prior* to the rite to set the mood; *during,* as an offering to the Goddess and God or to rouse energy; and *afterward* in pure celebration and joy. Some Wiccans compose a song that is in actuality a rite, encompassing everything from the creation of sacred space and invoking the deities to thanking them for their presence. Music magic is truly what you decide to make it.

Four distinct types of instruments have specific powers. The drum, rattle, xylophone, and all percussion instruments (save for the sistrum) are ruled by the element of *earth*. Thus, such instruments can be used to invoke fertifity, increase money, find a job, and so on. They can also be used to invoke the Goddess in ritual, or to "drum up" energy to send to the earth.

---

* A fine (if fictional) account of music magic can be found in chapter xi of Gerald Gardner's novel *High Magic's Aid* (New York: Weiser, 1975).

The flute, recorder, and all wind instruments are under the dominion of *air*, the intellectual element, and so can be used to increase mental powers or visualization abilities, to discover ancient wisdom or knowledge, to improve psychic faculties, and to call upon the God.

Fire rules stringed instruments such as the lyre, harp (full-size or folk), guitar, mandolin, ukelele, and so on. Such instruments can be used in spells or rites involving sexuality, health and bodily strength, passion and will power, change, evolution, courage, and the destruction of harmful habits.

They are also excellent tools to use before ritual to purify the area in question, and also the celebrant. Play a particular song, sing with the instrument, or just strum around the area in a clockwise circle until the place is humming with your vibrations. Strings can also be used to invoke the God.

Resonant metal such as the cymbal, sistrum, bell, and gong are symbolic of the element of *water*. Since water encompasses healing, fertility, friendship, psychic powers, spiritual love, beauty, compassion, happiness, and other similar energies—bells, gongs, or cymbals can be featured in such spells and rites. The sistrum of Isis reminds us that resonant metal invokes the Goddess.

Musical spells (as opposed to purely verbal spells) can be simple and effective. Need money? Sit quietly dressed in green and slowly thump a drum, visualizing yourself bursting with cash while invoking the Goddess in her aspect of provider-of-abundance.

If you're depressed, find a bell with a pleasant tone and ritually strike or ring it, feeling the sound's vibrations cleansing you of the depression and lifting your spirits. Or, wear a small bell.

When you're afraid, play a six-string guitar or listen to pre-recorded guitar music while visualizing yourself as confident and courageous. Invoke the God in his horned, aggressive, protective aspect.

Singing, a combination of speech and music, can be readily integrated into Wiccan rituals. Some Wiccans set chants and invocations to music or sing as they feel compelled to during ritual.

Many Wiccans never pursue the subject of music magic and simply play recorded tunes as backgrounds to their rituals. This is fine, but self-created music (however simple) integrated into your rituals can be more effective, as long as you like the piece.

Today a number of pre-recorded Wiccan and pagan cassette tapes are available. While widely varying in quality, it's worthwhile to pick up a few tapes by mail (see appendix I, "Occult Suppliers," for mail-order information). Some songs can be used in ritual, but most are best played while preparing for ritual, or afterward when relaxing.

Appropriate music incorporated into ritual can greatly enhance the Wiccan experience.

Dance

Dance is certainly an ancient ritual practice. It's also a magical act, for physical movement releases energy from the body, the same energy used in magic. This "secret" was discovered early, and so dance was incorporated into magic and ritual to raise energy, to alter consciousness, or simply to honor the Goddess and God with ritual performances.

Group dances, such as the spiral dance, are often performed in coven workings. In individual workings, however, you're bound by no tradition or choreographed steps. Feel free to move in any manner you wish, no matter how child-like or wild it may seem.

In magic, many Wiccans perform a short spell or ritual manipulation of some kind (inscribing runes, tying knots, tracing pictures in sand or powdered herbs, chanting deity names) and then perform the real magic: raising and channeling magical energy. They often move in an increasingly faster clockwise circle around the altar, either alone or with a coven, watching the candles flaming on the altar, smelling the incense, overwhelming themselves with chanting and intense visualization. When the practitioner has reached the point of no return, the exact moment when the body can raise and channel no more energy, the power is released toward the magical goal. To do this, some Wicca collapse to the ground, signaling the end of what is rather peculiarly called "The Dance."

Dancing is used to raise energy as well as to facilitate attunement with the deities of nature. Dance as the wild wind; as the stream rushing down a mountain, a flame flickering from a lightning-struck tree, as grains of sand bounding off each other in a gale, as flowers unfolding their brilliance on a sunny summer afternoon. As you dance, using whatever movements you wish, open yourself to the God and Goddess.

Think for a moment of the whirling dervishes, the untamed Gypsy dances of Europe, the sensuous belly dancing of the Middle East, and the sacred hula of old Hawaii. Dance is one of the paths to deity.

Gesture

Gestures are silent counterparts to words. Gestures can enhance Wiccan rituals when performed in conjunction with invocations or dance, or can be used alone for their real power. Pointing (as mentioned above), the use of the first and middle fingers splayed to create a "v," and the vulgar presentation of an upraised middle finger, demonstrate the variety of messages that can be conveyed through gesture, as well as the range of our emotional responses to them.

My introduction to Wicca happened to include some of these old gestures. In 1971 I saw some photographs* of magical protective gestures such as the *mano figa* (a hand clenched into a fist, the thumb jutting out between the first and middle fingers) and the *mano cornuta*, a "v" formed by the first and little fingers and held upside down. Both have long been used to avert the evil eye and negativity, and the latter is used in Wicca, with points up, to represent the God in his horned aspect.

A few days later, in my first year in high school, I flashed these two gestures to a girl I'd just met. There was no logical reason to do this; it just felt right. She looked at me, smiled, and asked me if I was a Witch. I said no, but I'd like to be. She began training me.

The magical significance of gestures is complex, and stems from the powers of the hand. The hand can heal or kill, caress or stab. It is a channel through which energies are sent from the body or received from others. Our hands set up our magical altars, grasp wands and athames, and pinch out candle flames at the conclusion of magical rites.

---

* Included in Douglas Hill and Pat William's *The Supernatural* (New York: Hawthorn Books, 1965), page 200.

Hands, as the means by which most of us earn our livings, are symbolic of the physical world. But in their five digits lie the pentagram, the supreme protective magical symbol; the sum of the four elements coupled with *akasha,* the spiritual power of the universe.

The lines on our hands can, to the trained, be used to link into the deep consciousnesses and reveal things to the conscious mind that we would otherwise have difficulty knowing. The palmist doesn't read these lines as streets on a roadmap; they are a key to our souls, a fleshy mandala revealing our innermost depths.

Hands were used as the first counting devices. They were seen to have both male and female qualities and symbolism, and images of hands were used around the world as amulets.

Gestures in Wiccan ritual can easily become second nature. When invoking the Goddess and God, the hands can be held uplifted with the fingers spread to receive their power. The Goddess can be individually invoked with the left hand, the thumb and first finger held up and curled into a half-circle, while the rest of the fingers are tucked against the palm. This represents the crescent moon. The God is invoked with the first and middle fingers of the right hand raised, or with the first and fourth fingers up, the thumb holding down the others against the palm, to represent horns.

The elements can be invoked with individual gestures when approaching the four directions: a flat hand held parallel with the ground to invoke earth at the north; an upraised hand, fingers spread wide apart, to invoke air at the east; an upraised fist for the south to invite fire, and a cupped hand to the west to invoke water.

Two gestures, together with postures, have long been used to invoke the Goddess and God, and are named after them. The Goddess position is assumed by placing the feet about two feet apart on the ground, holding the hands out, palms away from you, elbows bent slightly. This position can be used to call the Goddess or to attune with her energies.

The God position consists of the feet together on the floor, body held rigidly upright, arms crossed on the chest (right over left, usually), hands held in fists. Tools such as the wand and magic knife (athame) are sometimes held in the fists, echoing the practice of pharaohs of ancient Egypt who held a crook and flail in a similar position while trying disputes.

In coven work, the High Priestess and High Priest often assume these positions when invoking the Goddess and God. In solo workings they can be used to identify with the aspects of the Goddess and God within us, and also during separate invocatory rites.

Gestures are also used in magic. Each of the fingers relates to a specific planet as well as an ancient deity. Since pointing is a magical act and is a part of many spells, the finger can be chosen by its symbolism.

The thumb relates to Venus and to the planet Earth. Jupiter (both the planet and the god) rules the forefinger. The middle finger is ruled by the god and planet Saturn, the fourth finger the sun and Apollo, and the little finger by the planet Mercury as well as the god after which it is named.

Many spells involve pointing with the Jupiter and Saturn fingers, usually at an object to be charged or imbued with magical energy. The power is visualized as traveling straight out through the fingers and into the object.

Other ritual gestures used in Wiccan rites include the "cutting" of pentagrams at the four quarters by drawing them in the air with the magic knife, wand, or index finger. This is done to alternately banish or invoke elemental powers. It is, of course, performed with visualization.

The hand can be seen as a cauldron, since it can cup and contain water; an athame, since it is used to direct magical energy, and a wand, since it can also invoke.

Gestures are magical tools as potent as any other, ones we can always take with us, to be used when needed.

6

Ritual and Preparation for Ritual

I HAVE DEFINED ritual as "a specific form of movement, manipulation of objects, or series of inner processes designed to produce desired effects" (see glossary). In Wicca, rituals are ceremonies that celebrate and strengthen our relationships with the Goddess, the God, and the earth.

These rituals need not be preplanned, rehearsed, or traditional, nor must they slavishly adhere to one particular pattern or form. Indeed, Wiccans I've spoken with on the subject agree that spontaneously created rituals can be the most powerful and effective.

A Wiccan rite may consist of a lone celebrant lighting a fire, chanting sacred names, and watching the moonrise. Or it may involve ten or more people, some of whom assume various roles in mythic plays, or speak long passages in honor of the Gods. The rite may be ancient or newly written. Its outer form isn't important as long as it is successful in achieving an awareness of the deities within the Wiccan.

Wiccan ritual usually occurs on the nights of the full moon and the eight days of power, the old agricultural and seasonal festivals of Europe. Rituals are usually spiritual in nature but may also include magical workings.

In section III you'll find a complete book of rituals, *The Standing Stones Book of Shadows*. The best way to learn Wicca is to practice it; thus through the course of time, by performing rituals such as those in this book or the ones you write yourself, you'll gain an understanding of the true nature of Wicca.

Many people say they want to practice Wicca, but sit back and tell themselves that they can't observe the full moon with ritual because they don't have a teacher, aren't initiated, or don't know what to do.

These are merely excuses. If you're interested in practicing Wicca, simply do so.

To the lone Wiccan, the creation of new rituals can be an exciting practice. You might spend nights with reference works, piecing together bits of ritual and invocation, or simply allow the spirit of the moment and the wisdom of the deities to fill you with inspiration. No matter how they're created, all rituals should be done out of joy, not obligation.

If you wish, time your rites with the seasons, pagan feast days, and phases of the moon (For more on the subject, see chapter 8, "The Days of Power"). If you feel particularly attracted to other sacred calendars, feel free to adapt them. There have been highly successful adaptations of Wicca utilizing ancient Egyptian, American Indian, Hawaiian, Babylonian, and other religio-magical systems. Though most of Wicca has, until recently, been primarily European and British-based, this needn't limit us. We're free to do what we will as solitary Wiccans. So long as the rituals are fulfilling and effective, why worry?

Instructions on designing your own rituals are included in chapter 13, but some words regarding preparation for ritual are appropriate here.

First off, make sure you won't be interrupted during your religious (or magical) rite. If you're at home, tell your family that you'll be busy and aren't to be disturbed. If alone, take the phone off the hook, lock the doors, and pull the blinds, if you wish. It's best if you can ensure that you will be alone and undisturbed for some time.

A ritual bath commonly follows. For some time I almost couldn't bring myself to do a rite without having a quick dip first. This is partly psychological: if you feel clean and refreshed from the day's worries, you'll feel comfortable contacting the Goddess and God.

Ritual purification is a common feature among many religions. In Wicca, we see water as a purifying substance that strips off the disturbing vibrations of everyday tensions and allows us to stand before the deities with purity of body as well as purity of thought.

On a deeper level, immersion in water links us with our most primal memories. Bathing in a tub of cool, salted water is akin to walking into the waves of the ever-welcoming ocean, the domain of the Goddess. It prepares us spiritually and physically (have you ever felt different in the tub?) for the coming experience.

The bath often becomes a ritual itself. Candles can be burned in the bathroom, along with incense. Fragrant oils or herbal sachets can be added to the water. My favorite purification bath sachet consists of equal parts of rosemary, fennel, lavender, basil, thyme, hyssop, vervain, mint, with a touch of ground valerian root. (This formula is derived from *The Key of Solomon*.) Place this in a cloth, tie the ends up to trap the herbs inside, and pop it into the tub.

Outdoor rituals near the ocean or lakes and streams can begin with a quick swim. Of course, bathing isn't possible prior to spontaneous rituals. Even the necessity of ritual bathing is questioned by some. If you feel comfortable bathing, do so. If you don't feel it's necessary, it isn't.

Once bathed, it's time to dress for ritual. Among many Wiccans today (particularly those influenced by the writings and ideals of Gerald Gardner, or one of his students—see bibliography), nudity is a preferable state in which to invoke the deities of nature. It is certainly true that this is the most natural condition in which the human body can be, but ritual nudity isn't for everyone. The Church did much to instill shameful feelings regarding the undraped human figure. These distorted, unnatural emotions survive today.

Many reasons are given for this insistence on ritual nudity.* Some Wiccans state that the clothed body can't emit personal power as effectively as can a naked body, but then go on to say that when necessary, clothed rituals performed indoors are as effective as nude outdoor rites.

If clothed, Wiccans produce magic just as effective as that produced by naked Wiccans. Clothing is no barrier to the transference of power.

A more convincing explanation of Wiccan ritual nudity is that it is used for its symbolic value: mental, spiritual, as well as physical nudity before the Goddess and God symbolize the Wiccan's honesty and openness. Ritual nudity was practiced in many ancient religions and

---

* One of these that usually isn't stated is the most obvious: people like to look at naked bodies. Some unscrupulous persons form covens with the sole purpose of practicing social nudity. Such groups, it is readily apparent, aren't promoting the aims of Wicca: union of the Goddess and God and reverence for nature. I hasten to add that the majority of covens that practice ritual nudity aren't of this type.

can be found today in scattered areas of the world, so this isn't really a new idea, except to some westerners.

Though many covens insist on ritual nudity, you needn't worry about that. As a solitary practitioner the choice is yours. If you don't feel comfortable with ritual nudity, even in private, don't use it. There are many options.

Specialized dress, such as robes and tabards, are quite popular among some Wiccans. Various reasons are given for the use of robes, one of which is that slipping into garments worn only for magic lends a mystic atmosphere to such rituals and shifts your awareness to the coming proceedings, thereby promoting ritual consciousness.

Colors are also used for their specific vibrations. The listing below is a good sampling of robe colors. If I was especially interested in herb magic or performed rituals designed to halt the proliferation of nuclear power plants and weapons, I might wear a green robe to help key my rituals into earth energies. Specific robes can also be made and worn by the industrious for certain spells or cycles of spells, according to the descriptions below.

Yellow is an excellent color for those involved with divination.

Purple is favored for those who work with pure divine power (magicians) or who wish to deepen their spiritual awareness of the Goddess and God.

Blue is suited for healers and those who work with their psychic awareness or for attuning with the Goddess in her oceanic aspect.

Green empowers herbalists and magical ecologists.

Brown is worn by those who attune with animals or who cast spells for them.

White symbolizes purification and pure spirituality, and also is perfect for meditation and cleansing rituals. It is worn for full moon celebrations, or to attune with the Goddess.

Orange or **red** robes can be worn to sabbats, for protective rites, or when attuning with the God in his fiery solar aspect

Black robes are quite popular. Contrary to popular misconceptions, black doesn't symbolize evil. It is the absence of color. It is a protective hue and symbolizes the night, the universe, and a lack of falsehood. When a Wiccan wears a black robe, she or he is donning the blackness of outer space—symbolically, the ultimate source of divine energy.

If this is too complicated for you, simply make or buy one robe and wear it for every ritual.

Robes range from simple bath-type designs to fully hooded and lined monkish creations, complete with bell sleeves guaranteed to go up in flames if waved too close to candles. Some Wiccans wear robes with hoods, to shut off outside interference and to control sensory stimulation during ritual. This is a fine idea for magic or meditation but not for Wiccan religious rites, when we should be opening ourselves to nature rather than cutting off our connections with the physical world.

If you don't wish to dress in such a garment, are unable to sew, or simply can't find anyone to make one for you, just wear clean clothing of natural fibers such as cotton, wool, and silk.* So long as you're comfortable with what you are (or aren't) wearing, you're doing fine. Why not experiment to see what "suits" you best?

Selecting and donning ritual jewelry naturally follows dressing. Many Wiccans have collections of exotic pieces with religious or magical designs. Then, too, amulets and talismans (devices made to ward off or to attract forces) often double as ritual jewelry. Such wonders as necklaces of amber and jet, silver or gold bands worn on the wrists,

---

* I realize that this is a heretical statement. Many Wiccans become quite angry when I suggest this. Such a reaction is the product of traditional Wiccan training. I feel, however, that wearing clean street clothing during ritual is no more absurd than is doning the ubiquitous, hot, and uncomfortable robes that so many Wiccans seem to love. To each their own.

crowns of silver set with crescent moons, rings of emeralds and pearls, even ritual garters set with tiny silver buckles are often part of Wiccan regalia.

But you needn't purchase or make such extravagances. Keep it simple for now. If you feel comfortable wearing one or two pieces of jewelry during ritual, fine! Choose designs incorporating crescents, ankhs, five-pointed stars (pentagrams), and so on. Many mail-order suppliers carry occult jewelry. If you wish to reserve such pieces for ritual wear, fine. Many do.

I'm often asked if I have a good luck charm, a piece of jewelry, an amulet, or some other power object that I always have in my possession. I don't.

This often comes as a surprise, but it is part of my magical philosophy. If I determined that one piece of jewelry (a ring, pendant, quartz crystal point, etc.) was my power object, my link with the Gods, my assurance of good luck, I'd be crushed if it was stolen, lost, misplaced or otherwise parted company with me.

I could say that the power had gone out of it, that it was a magical lemon, taken by higher beings, or that I'm not as aware as I think. But I'd still be devastated.

It isn't wise to put our hopes, dreams, and energies into physical objects. This is a limitation, a direct product of the materialism fostered upon us all our lives. It's easy to say, "I can't do a thing since I lost my lucky moonstone necklace." It's also tempting to think, "Nothing's gone right since my horned God ring disappeared."

What *isn't* easy to see is that *all the power and luck we need is within ourselves.* It isn't wrapped up in exterior objects unless we allow it to be. If we do this, we leave ourselves open to losing that part of our personal power and good fortune, something I won't willingly do.

Power objects and ritual jewelry can indeed be reminders of the Goddess and God, and symbols of our own affinities. But I feel they shouldn't be allowed to become more than that.

Still, I do have a few pieces (a silver pentagram, an image of the Goddess, an Egyptian ankh, a Hawaiian fishhook that symbolizes the god Maui) that I sometimes wear during ritual. Donning such objects triggers the mind and produces that state of consciousness that is necessary for effective ritual.

I'm not saying that power shouldn't be sent into objects: indeed, this is the way magically charged talismans and amulets are made. I simply prefer not to do so with personal and ritual jewelry.

Certain natural objects, such as quartz crystals, are worn to invite their energies within ourselves to effect specific changes. This type of "power object" is a fine adjunct to personal energies—but it's dangerous to rely on them exclusively.

If wearing specific pieces puts you into a magical mood, or if wearing an image of the Goddess or one of her sacred symbols draws you closer to her, fine.

Your goal, however, should perhaps be the ability to constantly tune in on the hidden world around us and the reality of the Goddess and God, even in the midst of the most grounding, debasing follies of the human experience.

So, now you're bathed, clothed, adorned, and ready for ritual. Any other considerations? Yes, a big one—company.

Do you wish to worship the Old Gods of Wicca privately, or with others? If you have interested friends you may want to invite them to join you.

If not, no problem. Solo ritual is fine when starting out on the Wiccan way. The presence of like-minded people is wonderful, but can be inhibiting as well.

There are certainly rituals at which others can't be present. An unexpected glimpse of the full moon half-shrouded in clouds calls for a few moments of silence or attunement, an invocation, or meditation. These are all rituals shared with the Goddess and God alone. Deities don't stand on ceremony; they're as unpredictable and flowing as nature herself.

If you wish to gather with friends for your rituals, do so only with those who are truly in tune with your feelings concerning Wicca. Snickers and wandering thoughts will do nothing to further your Wiccan progress.

Also beware the love interest—the boyfriend or girlfriend, husband or wife who takes an interest only because you're interested. They may seem to be genuine, but after a while you may realize they're not contributing to the rituals.

There are many wonderful aspects to coven workings; I've experienced them. Most of the best of Wicca can be found in a good coven (and the worst in a bad one), but most people can't contact covens. They may also lack friends who are interested in practicing with them. This is the reason why I've written this book for solitary practitioners. If you wish, continue searching for a teacher or coven to train with while working with this book and other Wiccan guides. If you do meet someone, you'll be able to approach them with a practical knowledge of Wicca from personal experience, rather than mere book learning.

In spite of the emphasis placed on initiations and group workings in the vast majority of books on Wicca, solitary Wicca shouldn't be viewed as second best to the real thing. There are far more individuals worshipping the Old Ones today than there are coven members, and a surprising number of these work solo out of choice. Save for a few group meetings I attend each year, I'm one of them.

Never feel inferior because you're not working under the guidance of a teacher or an established coven. Don't worry that you won't be recognized as a true Wiccan. Such recognition is important only in the eyes of those giving or withholding it, otherwise it is meaningless.

You only need worry about pleasing yourself and developing a rapport with the Goddess and God. Feel free to write your own rituals. Break off the handcuffs of rigid conformity and the idea of "revealed books" that must be slavishly followed. Wicca is an evolving religion. A love of nature and the Goddess and God are at its heart, not unending tradition and ancient rites.

I'm not saying that traditional Wicca is bad. Far from it. Indeed, I've received initiation into several Wiccan traditions, each with their own rituals of initiation, sabbat and esbat observances (see chapter 8, "The Days of Power"), names for the Goddess and God, legends and magical lore. But after receiving these "secrets" I've come to realize that they're all the same, and the greatest secrets of all are available to anyone who takes the time to view nature as a manifestation of the Goddess and God.

Each tradition (expression) of Wicca, whether passed down or intuitively performed, is akin to a petal of a flower. No one petal constitutes the whole; all are necessary to the flower's existence. The solitary path is as much a part of Wicca as is any other.

7

The Magic Circle and the Altar

THE CIRCLE, MAGIC circle, or sphere is a well-defined though non-physical temple. In much of Wicca today, rituals and magical workings take place within such a construction of personal power.

The magic circle is of ancient origin. Forms of it were used in old Babylonian magic. Ceremonial magicians of the Middle Ages and the Renaissance also utilized them, as did various American Indian tribes, though not, perhaps, for the same reasons.

There are two main types of magic circles. Those used by ceremonial magicians of yesterday (and today) are designed to protect the magician from the forces which he or she raises. In Wicca, the circle is used to create a sacred space in which humans meet with the Goddess and God.

In pre-Christian Europe, most pagan religious festivals occurred outdoors. These were celebrations of the sun, moon, the stars, and of the earth's fertility. The standing stones, stone circles, sacred groves, and revered springs of Europe are remnants of those ancient days.

The pagan rites went underground when they were outlawed by the newly powerful Church. No longer did meadows know the sounds of voices chanting the old names of the sun gods, and the moon hung unadored in the nighttime skies.

The pagans grew secretive about their rites. Some practiced them outside only under the cover of darkness. Others brought them indoors.

Wicca has, unfortunately, inherited this last practice. Among many Wiccans, outdoor ritual is a novelty, a pleasant break from stuffy house-bound rites. I call this syndrome "living room Wicca." Though most Wiccans practice their religion indoors, it's ideal to run the rites outside beneath the sun and moon, in wild and lonely places far from the haunts of humans.

Such Wiccan rites are difficult to perform today. Traditional Wiccan rituals are complex and usually require a large number of tools. Privacy is also hard to find, and fear of merely being seen is another. Why this fear?

There are otherwise responsible, intelligent adults who would rather see us dead than practicing our religion. Such "Christians"* are few but they certainly do exist, and even today Wiccans are exposed to psychological harassment and physical violence at the hands of those who misunderstand their religion.

Don't let this scare you off. Rituals can be done outdoors, if they're modified so as to attract a minimum of attention. Wearing a black, hooded robe, stirring a cauldron, and flashing knives through the air in a public park isn't the best way to avoid undue notice.

Street clothing is advisable in the case of outdoor rituals in areas where you may be seen. Tools can be used, but remember that they're accessories, not necessities. Leave them at home if you feel that they'll become problems.

On a 1987 trip to Maui, I rose at dawn and walked to the beach. The sun was just rising behind Haleakala, tinting the ocean with pinks and reds. I wandered along the coral sand to a place where the warm water crashed against lava rocks.

There I set up a small stone in the sand in honor of the ancient Hawaiian deities. Sitting before it, I opened myself to the presence of the *akua* (gods and goddesses) around me. Afterward I walked into the ocean and threw a plumeria lei onto the water, offering it to Hina, Pélé, Laka, Kane, Lono, Kanaloa, and all their kin.†

I used no lengthy speeches and brandished no tools in the air. Still, the deities were there, all around, as the waves splashed against my legs

---

* I put quotes around this word for obvious reasons: such violent, crazed individuals certainly aren't Christians. Even Fundamentalists usually limit their activities to preaching and picketing—not violence, fire-bombing, and beatings.

† Or, as the Hawaiians would term them, the four thousand gods, the forty thousand gods, and the four hundred thousand gods. "Gods" here refers to deities and semi-divine beings of both genders.

and the sunrise broke fully over the ancient volcano, touching the sea with emerald light.

Outdoor rituals such as this can be a thousand times more effective *because they are outdoors,* not in a room filled with steel and plastic and the trappings of our technological age.

When these aren't possible (weather is certainly a factor), Wiccans transform their living rooms and bedrooms into places of power. They do this by creating sacred space, a magical environment in which the deities are welcomed and celebrated, and in which Wiccans become newly aware of the aspects of the God and Goddess within. Magic may also be practiced there. This sacred space is the magic circle.

It is practically a prerequisite for indoor workings. The circle defines the ritual area, holds in personal power, shuts out distracting energies—in essence, it creates the proper atmosphere for the rites. Standing within a magic circle, looking at the candles shining on the altar, smelling the incense and chanting ancient names is a wonderfully evocative experience. When properly formed and visualized, the magic circle performs its function of bringing us closer to the Goddess and God.

The circle is constructed with personal power that is felt (and visualized) as streaming from the body, through the magic knife, (athame) and out into the air. When completed, the circle is a sphere of energy that encompasses the entire working area. The word "circle" is a misnomer; a *sphere* of energy is actually created. The circle simply marks the ring where the sphere touches the earth (or floor) and continues on through it to form the other half.

Some kind of marking is often placed on the ground to show where the circle bisects the earth. This might be a cord lain in a roughly circular shape, a lightly drawn circle of chalk, or objects situated to show its outlines. These include flowers (ideal for spring and summer rites); pine boughs (winter festivals), stones or shells; quartz crystals, even tarot cards. Use objects that spark your imagination and are in tune with the ritual. (See chapter 13, Ritual Design, for more information regarding the magic circle.)

The circle is usually nine feet in diameter,* though any comfortable size is fine. The cardinal points are often marked with lit candles, or the ritual tools assigned to each point.

The pentacle, a bowl of salt, or earth may be placed to the north. This is the realm of earth, the stabilizing, fertile, and nourishing element that is the foundation of the other three.

The censer with smoldering incense is assigned to the east, the home of the intellectual element, air. Fresh flowers or stick incense can also be used. Air is the element of the mind, of communication, movement, divination, and ascetic spirituality.

To the south, a candle often represents fire, the element of transformation, of passion and change, success, health, and strength. An oil lamp or piece of lava rock may be used as well.

A cup or bowl of water can be placed in the west of the circle to represent water, the last of the four elements. water is the realm of the emotions, of the psychic mind, love, healing, beauty, and emotional spirituality.

Then again, these four objects may be placed on the altar, their positions corresponding to the directions and their elemental attributes.

Once the circle has been formed around the working space, rituals begin. During magical workings the air within the circle can grow uncomfortably hot and close—it will truly feel different from the outside world, charged with energy and alive with power.

The circle is a product of energy, a palpable construction that can be sensed and felt with experience. It isn't just a ring of flowers or a cord but a solid, viable barrier.

In Wiccan thought the circle represents the Goddess, the spiritual aspects of nature, fertility, infinity, and eternity. It also symbolizes the earth itself.

The altar, bearing the tools, stands in the center of the circle. It can be made of any substance, though wood is preferred. Oak is especially

---

* Nine is a number of the Goddess.

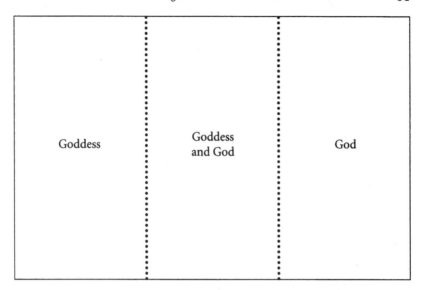

| Goddess | Goddess and God | God |

Symbolic divine areas of the altar

recommended for its power and strength, as is willow that is sacred to the Goddess.

The Wicca don't believe that the Goddess and God inhabit the altar itself. It is a place of power and magic, but it isn't sacrosanct. Though the altar is usually set up and dismantled for each magical ritual, some Wiccans have permanent home altars as well. Your shrine can grow into such an altar.

The altar is sometimes round, to represent the Goddess and spirituality, though it may also be square, symbolic of the elements. It may be nothing more than an area of ground, a cardboard box covered with cloth, two cinder blocks with a board lying on top, a coffee table, an old sawed-off tree stump in the wild, or a large, flat rock. During outdoor rituals, a fire may substitute for the altar. Stick incense may be used to outline the circle. The tools used are the powers of the mind.

The Wiccan tools are usually arranged upon the altar in a pleasing pattern. Generally, the altar is set in the center of the circle facing north. North is a direction of power. It is associated with the earth, and because this is our home we may feel more comfortable with this alignment. Then too, some Wiccans place their altars facing east, where the sun and moon rise.

The left half of the altar is usually dedicated to the Goddess. Tools sacred to her are placed there: the cup, the pentacle, bell, crystal, and cauldron. An image of the Goddess may also stand there, and a broom might be laid against the left side of the altar.*

If you can't find an appropriate Goddess image (or, simply, if you don't desire one), a green, silver, or white candle can be substituted. The cauldron is also sometimes placed on the floor to the left side of the altar if it is too large to fit on top.

To the right side, the emphasis is on the God. A red, yellow, or gold candle, or an appropriate figure, is usually placed there, as are the censer, wand, athame (magic knife), and white-handled knife.

Flowers may be set in the middle, perhaps in a vase or small cauldron. Then too, the censer is often centrally situated so that its smoke is offered up to both the Goddess and the God, and the pentacle might be placed before the censer.

Some Wiccans follow a more primitive, nature-oriented altar plan. To represent the Goddess, a round stone (pierced with a hole if available), a corn dolly, or a seashell work well. Pine cones, tapered stones, and acorns can be used to represent the God. Use your imagination in setting up the altar.

If you're working magic in the circle, all necessary items should be within it before you begin, either on the altar or beneath it. Never forget to have matches handy, and a small bowl to hold the used ones (it's impolite to throw them into the censer or cauldron).

Though we may setup images of the Goddess and God, we're not idol worshippers. We don't believe that a given statue or pile of rocks actually is the deity represented. And although we reverence nature, we don't worship trees or birds or stones. We simply delight in seeing them as manifestations of the universal creative forces—the Goddess and God.

---

* Some Wiccans—particularly those reclaiming women's spirituality—may also place a labrys (double-headed axe) there as well. The labrys is symbolic of the phases of the moon and of the Goddess. It was extensively used in Crete.

Goddess symbol or candle	Censer	God symbol or candle
Bowl of water	Red candle	Bowl of salt
Cup		Incense
	Pentacle	
Crystal		Knife/ wand
	Cauldron, or spell materials	
Bell		Bolline

Suggested altar layout

The altar and the magic circle in which it stands is a personal construction and it should be pleasing to you. My first Wiccan teacher laid out elaborate altars attuned with the occasion—if we couldn't practice outdoors. For one full moon rite she draped the altar with white satin, placed white candles in crystal holders, added a silver chalice, white roses, and snowy-leafed dusty miller. An incense composed of white roses, sandalwood, and gardenias drifted through the air. The glowing altar suffused the room with lunar energies. Our ritual that night was one to remember.

May yours be the same.

8

The Days of Power

IN THE PAST, when people lived with nature, the turning of the seasons and the monthly cycle of the moon had a profound impact on religious ceremonies. Because the moon was seen as a symbol of the Goddess, ceremonies of adoration and magic took place in its light. The coming of winter, the first stirrings of spring, the warm summer, and the advent of fall were also marked with rituals.

The Wiccans, heirs of the pre-Christian folk religions of Europe, still celebrate the full moon and observe the changing of the seasons. The Wiccan religious calendar contains thirteen full moon celebrations and eight sabbats or days of power.

Four of these days (or, more properly, nights) are determined by the solstices and equinoxes,* the astronomical beginnings of the seasons. The other four ritual occasions are based on old folk festivals (and, to some extent, those of the ancient Middle East). The rituals give structure and order to the Wiccan year, and also remind us of the endless cycle that will continue long after we're gone.

Four of the sabbats—perhaps those that have been observed for the longest time—were probably associated with agriculture and the bearing cycles of animals. These are *Imbolc* (February 2), *Beltane* (April 30), *Lughnasadh* (August 1), and *Samhain* (October 31). These names are Celtic and are quite common among Wiccans, though many others exist.

---

* Traces of this old custom are even found in Christianity. Easter, for example, is placed on the Sunday following the first full moon after the spring equinox, a rather "pagan" way to organize religious rites.

When careful observation of the skies led to common knowledge of the astronomical year, the solstices and equinoxes (circa March 21, June 21, September 21, and December 21; the actual dates vary from year to year) were brought into this religious structure.*

Who first began worshipping and raising energy at these times? That question can't be answered. These sacred days and nights, however, are the origins of the twenty-one Wiccan ritual occasions.

Many of these survive today in both secular and religious forms. May Day celebrations, Halloween, Groundhog Day, and even Thanksgiving, to name some popular American holidays, are all connected with ancient pagan worship. Heavily Christianized versions of the sabbats have also been preserved within the Catholic Church.

The sabbats are solar rituals, marking the points of the sun's yearly cycle, and are but half of the Wiccan ritual year. The esbats are the Wiccan full moon celebrations. At this time we gather to worship She Who Is. Not that Wiccans omit the God at esbats—both are usually revered on all ritual occasions.

There are twelve to thirteen full moons yearly, or one every twenty-eight days. The moon is a symbol of the Goddess as well as a source of energy. Thus, after the religious aspects of the esbats, Wiccans often practice magic, tapping into the larger amounts of energy that are thought to exist at these times.

Some of the old pagan festivals, stripped of their once sacred qualities by the dominance of Christianity, have degenerated. Samhain seems to have been taken over by candy manufacturers in the United States, while Yule has been transformed from one of the most holy pagan days to a time of gross commercialism. Even the later echoes of a Christian savior's birth are hardly audible above the electronic hum of cash registers.

But the old magic remains on these days and nights, and the Wicca celebrate them. Rituals vary greatly, but all relate to the Goddess and God and to our home, the earth. Most rites are held at night for practical purposes as well as to lend a sense of mystery. The sabbats, being solar

---

* Solstices, equinoxes, and the sabbats are listed in *Llewellyn's Astrological Calendar*.

oriented, are more naturally celebrated at noon or at dawn, but this is rare today.

The sabbats tell us one of the stories of the Goddess and God, of their relationship and the effects this has on the fruitfulness of the earth. There are many variations on these myths, but here's a fairly common one, woven into basic descriptions of the sabbats.

Yule

The Goddess gives birth to a son, the God, at Yule (circa December 21). This is in no way an adaptation of Christianity. The winter solstice has long been viewed as a time of divine births. Mithras was said to have been born at this time. The Christians simply adopted it for their use in 273 C.E. (Common Era).

Yule is a time of the greatest darkness and is the shortest day of the year. Earlier peoples noticed such phenomena and supplicated the forces of nature to lengthen the days and shorten the nights. Wiccans sometimes celebrate Yule just before dawn, then watch the sunrise as a fitting finale to their efforts.

Since the God is also the sun, this marks the point of the year when the sun is reborn as well. Thus, the Wicca light fires or candles to welcome the sun's returning light. The Goddess, slumbering through the winter of her labor, rests after her delivery.

Yule is the remnant of early rituals celebrated to hurry the end of winter and the bounty of spring, when food was once again readily available. To contemporary Wiccans it is a reminder that the ultimate product of death is rebirth, a comforting thought in these days of unrest. (See chapter 9, "The Spiral of Rebirth.")

Imbolc

Imbolc (February 2) marks the recovery of the Goddess after giving birth to the God. The lengthening periods of light awaken her. The God is a young, lusty boy, but his power is felt in the longer days. The warmth fertilizes the earth (the Goddess), causing seeds to germinate and sprout. And so the earliest beginnings of spring occur.

This is a sabbat of purification after the shut-in life of winter, through the renewing power of the sun. It is also a festival of light and of fertility, once marked in Europe with huge blazes, torches, and fire in every form. Fire here represents our own illumination and inspiration as much as light and warmth.

Imbolc is also known as Feast of Torches, Oimelc, Lupercalia, Feast of Pan, Snowdrop Festival, Feast of the Waxing Light, Brigid's Day, and probably by many other names. Some female Wiccans follow the old Scandinavian custom of wearing crowns of lit candles,* but many more carry tapers during their invocations.

This is one of the traditional times for initiations into covens, and so self-dedication rituals, such as the one outlined in chapter 12, can be performed or renewed at this time.

Ostara

Ostara (circa March 21), the spring equinox, also known as spring, Rites of Spring, and Eostra's Day, marks the first day of true spring. The energies of nature subtly shift from the sluggishness of winter to the exuberant expansion of spring. The Goddess blankets the earth with fertility, bursting forth from her sleep, as the God stretches and grows to maturity. He walks the greening fields and delights in the abundance of nature.

On Ostara the hours of day and night are equal. Light is overtaking darkness; the Goddess and God impel the wild creatures of the earth to reproduce.

This is a time of beginnings, of action, of planting spells for future gains, and of tending ritual gardens.

---

* See pages 101–102 of *Buckland's Complete Book of Witchcraft* (Llewellyn, 1986 and 2002) for details.

Beltane

Beltane (April 30) marks the emergence of the young God into manhood. Stirred by the energies at work in nature, he desires the Goddess. They fall in love, lie among the grasses and blossoms, and unite. The Goddess becomes pregnant of the God. The Wiccans celebrate the symbol of her fertility in ritual.

Beltane (also known as May Day) has long been marked with feasts and rituals. May poles, supremely phallic symbols, were the focal point of old English village rituals. Many persons rose at dawn to gather flowers and green branches from the fields and gardens, using them to decorate the May pole, their homes, and themselves.

The flowers and greenery symbolize the Goddess; the May pole the God. Beltane marks the return of vitality, of passion and hopes consummated.

May poles are sometimes used by Wiccans today during Beltane rituals, but the cauldron is a more common focal point of ceremony. It represents, of course, the Goddess—the essence of womanhood, the end of all desire, the equal but opposite of the May pole, symbolic of the God.

Midsummer

Midsummer, the summer solstice (circa June 21), also known as Litha, arrives when the powers of nature reach their highest point. The earth is awash in the fertility of the Goddess and God.

In the past, bonfires were leapt to encourage fertility, purification, health, and love. The fire once again represents the sun, feted on this time of the longest daylight hours.

Midsummer is a classic time for magic of all kinds.

Lughnasadh

Lughnasadh (August 1) is the time of the first harvest, when the plants of spring wither and drop their fruits or seeds for our use as well as to ensure future crops. Mystically, so too does the God lose his strength as the sun rises farther in the south each day and the nights grow longer. The Goddess watches in sorrow and joy as she realizes that the God is dying, and yet lives on inside her as her child.

Lughnasadh, also known as August Eve, Feast of Bread, Harvest Home, and Lammas, wasn't necessarily observed on this day. It originally coincided with the first reapings.

As summer passes, Wiccans remember its warmth and bounty in the food we eat. Every meal is an act of attunement with nature, and we are reminded that nothing in the universe is constant.

Mabon

Mabon (circa September 21), the autumn equinox, is the completion of the harvest begun at Lughnasadh. Once again day and night are equal, poised as the God prepares to leave his physical body and begin the great adventure into the unseen, toward renewal and rebirth of the Goddess.

Nature declines, draws back its bounty, readying for winter and its time of rest. The Goddess nods in the weakening sun, though fire burns within her womb. She feels the presence of the God even as he wanes.

Samhain

At Samhain (October 31), the Wicca say farewell to the God. This is a temporary farewell. He isn't wrapped in eternal darkness, but readies to be reborn of the Goddess at Yule.

Samhain, also known as November Eve, Feast of the Dead, Feast of Apples, Hallows and All Hallows, once marked the time of sacrifice. In some places this was the time when animals were slaughtered to ensure food throughout the depths of winter. The God—identified with the animals—fell as well to ensure our continuing existence.*

Samhain is a time of reflection, of looking back over the last year, of coming to terms with the one phenomenon of life over which we have no control—death. The Wicca feel that on this night the separation between the physical and spiritual realities is thin. Wiccans remember their ancestors and all those who have gone before.

After Samhain, Wiccans celebrate Yule, and so the wheel of the year is complete.

Surely there are mysteries buried here. Why is the God the son, and then the lover of the Goddess? This isn't incest, this is symbolism. In this agricultural story (one of many Wiccan myths) the ever-changing fertility of the earth is represented by the Goddess and God. This myth speaks of the mysteries of birth, death, and rebirth. It celebrates the wondrous aspects and beautiful effects of love, and honors women who perpetuate our species. It also points out the very real dependence that humans have on the earth, the sun, and the moon and of the effects of the seasons on our daily lives.

To agricultural peoples, the major thrust of this myth cycle is the production of food through the interplay between the Goddess and God. Food—without which we would all die—is intimately connected with the deities. Indeed, Wiccans see food as yet another manifestation of divine energy.

And so, by observing the sabbats, Wiccans attune themselves to the earth and to the deities. They reaffirm their earth roots. Performing rituals on the nights of the full moon also strengthens their connections with the Goddess in particular.

It is the wise Wiccan who celebrates on the sabbats and esbats, for these are times of real as well as symbolic power. Honoring them in some fashion—perhaps with rites similar to those suggested in *The Standing Stones Book of Shadows*—is an integral part of Wicca.

---

* Vegetarian Wiccans probably don't like this part of Samhain symbolism, but it is traditional. We don't, of course, sacrifice animals in ritual. This is symbolic of the God's passing.

9

The Spiral of Rebirth

REINCARNATION SEEMS TO be one of the most controversial spiritual topics of our time. Hundreds of books are being published on the subject as if the western world had only recently discovered this ancient doctrine.

Reincarnation is one of Wicca's most valuable lessons. The knowledge that this life is but one of many, that when the physical body dies we do not cease to exist, but are reborn in another body, answers many questions, but raises a few more.

Why? Why are we reincarnated? In common with many other religions, Wicca teaches that reincarnation is the instrument through which our souls are perfected. One lifetime isn't sufficient to attain this goal; hence, the consciousness (soul) is reborn many times, each life encompassing a different set of lessons, until perfection is achieved.

No one can say how many lives are required before this is accomplished. We are human and it's easy to fall into non-evolutionary behavior. Greed, anger, jealousy, obsession, and all our negative emotions inhibit our growth.

In Wicca, we seek to strengthen our bodies, minds, and souls. We certainly live full, productive, earthly lives, but we try to do so while harming none, the antithesis of competition, intimidation, and looking out for number one.

The soul is ageless, sexless, nonphysical, possessed of the divine spark of the Goddess and God. Each manifestation of the soul (i.e., each body it inhabits on earth) is different. No two bodies or lives are the same. If this wasn't so, the soul would stagnate. The sex, race, place of birth, economic class, and every other individuality of the soul is determined by its actions in past lives and the lessons necessary to the present.

This is of utmost importance in Wiccan thought: we decide the lay of our lives. There's no god or curse or mysterious force of fate upon which we can thrust the responsibility for the trials in our lives. We decide what we need to learn in order to evolve, and then, it is hoped, during incarnation, work toward this progress. If not, we regress into darkness.

As an aid in learning the lessons of each life, a phenomenon exists that has been called karma. Karma is often misunderstood. It is not a system of rewards and punishments, but a phenomenon that guides the soul toward evolving actions. Thusly, if a person performs negative actions, negative actions will be returned. Good brings good. With this in mind, there's little reason to act negatively.

Karma means action, and that's how it works. It is a tool, not a punishment. There's no way one can "wipe out" karma, and neither is every seemingly terrible event in our lives a byproduct of karma.

We learn from karma only when we're aware of it. Many look into their past lives to discover their mistakes, to uncover the problems inhibiting progress in this one. Trance and meditation techniques can help here, but true self-knowledge is the best means of accomplishing this.

Past-life regression can be a dangerous thing, for much self-delusion exists here. I can't tell you how many Cleopatras, King Arthurs, Merlins, Marys, Nefertitis, and other famous persons of the past I've met walking around in high-top tennis shoes and jeans. Our conscious minds, seeking past incarnations, easily hold onto such romantic ideals.

If this becomes a problem, if you don't wish to know your past lives, or lack the means to discover them, look at this life. You can learn everything of relevance about your past lives by examining this life. If you've cleared up problems in previous existences, they're of no concern to you today. If you haven't, the same problems will reappear, so look at this life.

At night, study your day's action, noting both positive, helpful actions and thoughts, as well as the negative. Then look at the past week, the past year, the past decade. Refer to diaries, journals, or old letters if you've kept them to refresh your memory. Do you continually make the same mistakes? If so, vow to never repeat them in a ritual of your own design.

At your altar or shrine, you might write such mistakes on a piece of paper. Your entries could include negative emotions, fear, indulgence without balance, allowing others to control your life, endless love-obsessions with men or women who are indifferent to your feelings. As you write these, visualize yourself doing these things in the past, not the present.

Then, light a red candle. Hold the paper in its flame and throw it into a cauldron or some other heat-proof container. Scream or shout— or simply affirm to yourself—that such past actions are no longer a part of you. Visualize your future life devoid of such harmful, limiting, inhibiting behavior. Repeat the spell as necessary, perhaps on nights of the waning moon, to finalize the destruction of these negative aspects of your life.

If you ritualize your determination to progress in this life, your vow will vibrate with strength. When you're tempted to fall into your old, negative modes of thinking or action, recall the ritual and overcome the urge with its power.

What happens after death? Only the body dies. The soul lives on. Some Wiccans say that it journeys to a realm variously known as the Land of the Faerie, the Shining Land, and the Land of the Young.* This realm is neither in heaven nor the underworld. It simply is—a nonphysical reality much less dense than ours. Some Wiccan traditions describe it as a land of eternal summer, with grassy fields and sweet flowing rivers, perhaps the earth before the advent of humans. Others see it vaguely as a realm without forms, where energy swirls

---

* These are Celtic terms. Some Wiccans call this place Summerland, which is a Theosophical term.

coexist with the greatest energies—the Goddess and God in their celestial identities.

The soul is said to review the past life, perhaps through some mysterious way with the deities. This isn't a judgment, a weighing of one's soul, but an incarnational review. Lessons learned or ignored are brought to light.

After the proper time, when the conditions on earth are correct, the soul is reincarnated and life begins again.

The final question—what happens after the last incarnation?

Wiccan teachings have always been vague on this. Basically, the Wiccans say that after rising upon the spiral of life and death and rebirth, those souls who have attained perfection break away from the cycle forever and dwell with the Goddess and God. Nothing is ever lost. The energies resident in our souls return to the divine source from which they originally emanated.

Because of their acceptance of reincarnation, the Wicca don't fear death as a final plunge into oblivion, the days of life on earth forever behind them. It is seen as the door to birth. Thus our very lives are symbolically linked with the endless cycles of the seasons that shape our planet.

Don't try to force yourself to believe in reincarnation. Knowledge is far superior to belief, for belief is the way of the uninformed. It isn't wise to accept a doctrine as important as reincarnation without a great deal of study to see if it speaks to you.

Also, though there may be strong connections with loved ones, be wary of the idea of soul mates, i.e., people you've loved in other lives and are destined to love again. Though your feelings and beliefs may be sincere, they aren't always based on fact. In the course of your life you might meet five or six other people with whom you feel the same tie, despite your current involvement. Can they all be soul mates?

One of the difficulties of this concept is that if we're all inextricably tied up with other persons' souls, if we continue to incarnate with them, we're learning absolutely nothing. Therefore, announcing that you've found your soul mate is rather akin to stating that you're not progressing on the incarnational spiral.*

One day you may know, not believe, that reincarnation is as real as a plant that buds, flowers, drops its seed, withers, and creates a new plant in its image. Reincarnation was probably first intuited by earlier peoples watching nature.

Until you've decided for yourself, you may wish to reflect upon and consider the doctrine of reincarnation.

---

* I realize I'm in dangerous water here again. Still, I've met many, many people who've made such announcements—only to tell me privately, "Boy, was I wrong."

10

Concerning Initiation

MOST SHAMANIC AND magical religions utilize some sort of initiation ceremony whereby an outsider becomes a recognized member of the religion, society, group, or coven. Such rites also mark the new direction that the initiate's life is taking.

Much has been made, publicly and privately, of Wiccan initiations. Each Wiccan tradition uses its own initiation ceremonies, which may or may not be recognized by other Wiccans. On one point, how-ever, most initiates agree: a person can be a Wiccan only if she or he has received such an initiation.

This brings up an interesting question: Who initiated the first Wiccan?

Most initiation ceremonies are nothing more than rites marking the acceptance of the person into a coven, and her or his dedication to the Goddess and God. Sometimes "power is passed" between the initiator and neophyte as well.

To a non-Wiccan, the initiation might seem to be a rite of conversion. This isn't the case. Wicca has no need for such rites. We don't condemn the deities with which we may have attuned before practicing Wicca, nor need we turn our backs on them.

The initiation ceremony (or ceremonies, since in many groups three successive rites are performed) is held to be of utmost importance to those Wiccan groups still practicing ritual secrecy. Surely anyone entering such a group should undergo an initiation, part of which consists of swearing never to reveal their secrets. This makes sense, and is a part of many coven initiations. But it isn't the essence of initiation.

Many people have told me that they desperately need to undergo Wiccan initiation. They seem to believe that one cannot practice Wicca without this stamp of approval. If you've read this far, you know that such isn't the case.

Wicca has been, up until the past decade or so, a closed religion, but no more. The inner components of Wicca are available to anyone who can read and understand the material. Wicca's only secrets are its individual ritual forms, spells, names of deities, and so on.

This needn't bother you. For every secret Wiccan ritual or Goddess name there are dozens (if not hundreds) of others published and readily available. At this moment, more Wiccan information has been released than ever before. While it once may have been a secret religion, today Wicca is a religion with few secrets.*

Still, many cling to the idea of the necessity of initiation, probably thinking that with this magical act they'll be granted the *secrets of the universe* and *untold power*. To make things worse, some particularly narrow-minded Wiccans say that the Goddess and God won't listen to anyone who isn't an athame-carrying member of a coven. Many would-be Wiccans believe this.

It doesn't work this way.

True initiation isn't a rite performed by one human being upon another. Even if you accept the concept that the initiator is suffused with deity during initiation, it's still just a ritual.

Initiation is a process, gradual or instantaneous, of the individual's attunement with the Goddess and God. Many of the Wicca readily admit that the ritual initiation is the outer form only. True initiation will often occur weeks or months later, or prior to, the physical ritual.

Since this is so, "real" Wiccan initiation may take place years before the student contacts a Wiccan coven or teacher. Is this initiation less effective or less genuine because the person hasn't gone through a formal ritual at the hands of another human being? Of course not.

---

* Some groups simply write their own "secret" Book of Shadows and restrict access to it. This does, indeed, ensure that it's secret—but not older or better than any other.

Rest assured, it's quite possible to experience a true Wiccan initiation without ever meeting another soul involved in the religion. You may even be unaware of it. Your life may gradually shift in focus until you realize that you notice the birds and clouds. You may gaze at the moon on lonely nights and talk to plants and animals. Sunset might bring a time of quiet contemplation.

Or you may change as the seasons change, adapting your body's energies to match those of the natural world around you. The Goddess and God may sing in your thoughts, and you may perform rituals before actually realizing what you're doing.

When the Old Ways have become a part of your life and your relationship with the Goddess and God is strong, when you have gathered your tools and performed the rites and magic out of joy, you are truly of the spirit and can rightly call yourself "Wiccan."

This may be your goal, or you may wish to stretch yourself further, perhaps continuing your search for an instructor. This is fine. But if you never find one, you'll have the satisfaction of knowing that you didn't sit around waiting for the mysteries to fall into your lap. You'll have worked the old magic and talked to the Goddess and God, reaffirming your commitment to the earth for spiritual evolvement, and transformed the lack of physical initiation into a positive stimulus to change your life and mode of thinking.

If you contact a teacher or coven, they'll probably find you're a student worthy of acceptance. But if you discover that you're not suited to their style of Wicca, or if your personalities clash, don't be crushed. You've still got your own Wicca to fall back upon as you continue your search.

This can be a lonely path, because so few of us follow the Old Ways. It's disheartening to spend your time reverencing nature and watching the earth suffocating under tons of concrete while nobody seems to care.

To contact others of like mind, you may wish to subscribe to Wiccan publications and start correspondence with Wiccans around the country. Continue to read new books as they're published on both Wicca and the Goddess. Keep up on the happenings in the Wiccan world. Collect and write new rituals and spells. Wicca need never grow stale.

Many wish to formalize their life within Wicca with a self-initiation ceremony. I've included one in section II for those who feel the need for it. Again, this is simply one way to do this. Improvise if you so desire.

If you decide to invite friends and interested people to join your rites, don't make them hang back and watch while you play "priestess" or "Witch." Involve them. Make them a part of the rites and magic. Use your imagination and practical experience to integrate them into the rituals.

When you feel an insurmountable joy in watching the sunset or the moon rise, when you see the Goddess and God in trees marching along mountains or streams meandering through fields, when you feel the pulsating energies of the earth amidst a noisy city, you have received true initiation and are linked with the ancient powers and ways of the deities.

Some say, "Only a Wiccan can make a Wiccan." I say only the Goddess and God can make a Wiccan. Who's better qualified?

Section II

Practice

11

Exercises and Magical Techniques

FOLLOWING ARE SHORT sections on various exercises and procedures that are vital to your growth in Wicca and magic. Such activities, which consume no more than a few minutes of each day, shouldn't be underestimated. They're the building blocks upon which fluency in all Wiccan and magical rites will be gained.

Making them a part of your everyday schedule allows you to grow day by day.

The Mirror Book

Right now, as soon as you finish reading this perhaps, begin a "mirror book." This is a magical record of your progress in Wicca. It can be anything from a locked diary to a spiral-bound notebook. In it, record all thoughts and feelings about Wicca, the results of your readings, magical successes and failures, doubts and fears, significant dreams— even mundane concerns. This book is for your eyes only. No one else need ever read it.

This book is a mirror of your spiritual life. As such it is quite valuable in assessing your progress in Wicca and life itself. Thus, when reading over the book, you become your own teacher. Notice problem areas and take steps to resolve them.

I've found the best time to record such information is directly before sleep. Date each entry and, if you wish, also include the moon's phase and any astronomical information that might be pertinent (lunar phases, eclipses, weather).

One of the goals of the Wicca is self-knowledge; the Mirror Book is a valuable tool in achieving this.

Breathing

Breathing is usually an unconscious act that we perform continuously throughout our lives. In magic and Wicca, however, breath can also be a tool for disciplining our bodies and entering into alternate states of consciousness.

In order to meditate correctly, you must breathe correctly. This is the most basic of exercises and, fortunately, is also the easiest.

Deep breathing techniques require the full use of the lungs as well as of the diaphragm. The diaphragm is located about two finger-widths below the rib cage. As you breathe in, push out with this region. Notice how much more air you can intake.

For breathing exercises, assume a comfortable position, either sitting or lying down (although deep breathing is possible in nearly every position). Relax your body slightly. Inhale through your nose to a slow count of three, four, or five—whatever is comfortable. Remember to allow the air to fill your diaphragm as well as your lungs. Retain the air, then exhale to the same slow count.

Repeat this several times, gradually slowing your breath rate. Never hold your breath past the level of comfort. The inhalation, retaining, and exhalation should be controlled, calm, and free of tension.

Concentrate on your breathing process while doing this. As you inhale, breathe in love, health, tranquility, perhaps visualizing (see "Visualization," page 88) these positive energies as golden-flecked air. In exhaling, breathe out hate, disease, anger, maybe visualizing black smoke exiting your lungs.

Oxygen is the breath of life and is necessary to our existence. Breathe properly and you'll be a better person and a better Wiccan. Deep breathing is used before every act of worship or magic, and is a part of concentration and visualization exercises. Breathe deeply when you feel anger exploding within you. Exhale the fury and inhale peace. It works every time—if you allow it to.

Practice deep breathing exercises daily, and gradually increase your capacity to retain air. It is wise, if possible, to occasionally practice this near the sea or in a forest, far from the polluted air of our cities. Deep breathing in these natural settings is not only more peaceful— it's also healthier.

Meditation

Meditation is an important art for inducing total relaxation. Too few of us find a moment of freedom from tensions and worries, so meditation is a welcome relief from the cares and frustrations of everyday living. More importantly, it's a quiet time in which we commune with the Goddess, the God, and ourselves, relaxing the conscious mind's hold on our psychic awareness. Meditation usually precedes every magical act and rite of worship.

Sitting is the ideal position for meditation, especially for those who tend to fall asleep during this practice.

Sit in a straight-backed chair, supporting your lower back with a pillow, if necessary. Your chin should be level with the floor, eyes closed, back straight, hands resting on your knees, palms up, and fingers relaxed. In this position you should be comfortable and relaxed, the spine straight, and the torso erect. If you have poor posture, it may be some time before this position becomes comfortable. Persevere.

Breathe deeply for several minutes. Relax. Forget. Visualize the multitude of tensions and worries of your everyday life exiting your body with your breath. Relax into the chair.

Now open your consciousness. Allow your conscious mind to be receptive and alert. Commune and talk with the deities. Toss around symbols in your head. If you wish, chant one of the names of the Goddess or God, or a group of them. This is an excellent tool for slipping into the twilight world.

Select your time and place for meditation with care. Light should be subdued; candlelight is excellent. Burn white or blue candles if you wish. A bit of incense is fine too, but too much smoke can (obviously) cause problems during deep breathing.

Immediately after each meditation, record all images, thoughts, and sensations in your mirror book.

Visualization

This is the most basic and yet advanced technique called for in magic and Wicca. The art of using our brains to "see" what is not physically present is a powerful magical tool used in many Wiccan rituals. For instance, the forming of the magic circle relies in part on the Wiccan's ability to visualize personal power flowing out to form a sphere of glowing light around the ritual area. This visualization, then, directs the power that actually creates the circle; it doesn't create it alone.

Because of its usefulness in changing our attitudes and lives, many books are being written on visualization today. Each book promises to show the secrets of visualization.

Fortunately, nearly all of us already possess this ability. It may not be fine-tuned, but practice makes perfect.

Can you, at this moment, see in your mind your best friend's face, or your least-favorite actor? What about the piece of clothing you most often wear, the exterior of your home, your car, or your bathroom?

That's visualization. Visualization is the act of seeing with the mind, not the eyes. Magical visualization is seeing something that is presently nonexistent. It may be a magic circle, a healed friend, an empowered talisman.

We can raise energy from our bodies, visualize it streaming out from our palms, and then form it into a small glowing sphere, fashioning it *physically* as if into a snowball, and *mentally* by seeing it as we desire.

In magic, I might raise energy and, while doing this, hold an image in my mind of something I need—a new car, for example. I visualize the car, see myself signing the contract to buy it, driving it on the road, pumping gas into its tank, and making payments. Then I direct energy to empower the visualization—to bring it into manifestation.

In other words, visualization "programs" the power. This could be explained as a form of mental sympathetic magic. Instead of creating a physical image, we create pictures in our heads.

Thoughts are definitely things. Our thoughts affect the quality of our lives. If we constantly moan about being broke, then do a fifteen-minute visualization to bring money into our lives, that fifteen minutes of energy will have to counteract twenty-three hours and forty-five minutes of daily, self-induced, negative programming. Thus we must keep our thoughts in order and in line with our desires and needs. Visualization can help here. To hone this tool, try these simple exercises, widely known within Wicca.

Exercise one: Sit or lie comfortably with your eyes shut. Relax your body. Breathe deeply and still your mind. Pictures will continue to pop into your head. Choose one of these and stick with it. Let no images intrude other than the one you've chosen. Keep all thoughts revolving around the image. Retain this picture for as long as you can, then let it go and end the exercise. When you can retain one picture for more than a few minutes, move on to the next step.

Exercise two: Decide upon an image to hold and retain it within your mind. You might wish to have it physically present and study it first, memorizing each detail—the way shadows play on it, its textures, colors, perhaps even a scent. You might choose a small, three-dimensional shape, such as a pyramid, or something more complex such as an image of Aphrodite rising from the sea or a ripe apple.

After studying it thoroughly, close your eyes and see the object before them—just as if your eyes were open. Don't look at the object again with your physical eyes but with your magical imagination—with your powers of visualization.

When you can hold this image perfectly for five minutes, move on.

Exercise three: This is more difficult, and is truly magical in nature. Visualize something, anything, but preferably something you've never seen. For instance, let's use a vegetable from Jupiter. It's purple, square, a foot across, covered with quarter-inch green hairs and half-inch yellow dots. This is just an example, of course.

Now close your eyes and see—*really see* this vegetable in your mind. It's never existed. You're creating it with your visualization, your magical imagination. Make the vegetable real. Turn it over in your mind so that you can see it from all angles. Then let it vanish.

When you can hold any such self-created image for about five minutes or so, continue on to the next exercise.

Exercise four: This is the most difficult. Hold a self-created image (such as the Jupiterian vegetable) in your mind *with your eyes open*. Work at keeping it visible, real, a palpable thing. Stare at a wall, look at the sky, or gaze at a busy street, but see that vegetable there. Make it so real you can touch it. Try having it resting on a table or sitting on the grass beneath a tree.

If we're to use visualization to create changes in this world, not in the shadowy realm that exists behind our eyelids, we must practice such techniques with our eyes open. The true test of visualization lies in our ability to make the visualized object (or structure) real and a part of our world. When you've perfected this exercise, you're well on the way.

Energy Play

The energy and magical powers at work in Wicca are real. They aren't of some astral plane. They're within the earth and ourselves. They maintain life. We daily deplete our store of energy and replenish it through the air we breathe, the food we eat, and the powers that stream down from the sun and moon.

Know that this power is physical. Yes, it's mysterious, but only because so few investigate it in magical ways. Following are some exercises to help you do just that. (You might wish to re-read chapter 3, "Magic.")

Calm yourself. Breathe deeply. Rub your palms together for twenty seconds. Start slowly and rub faster and faster. Feel your muscles tense. Feel your palms grow warm. Then, suddenly, stop and hold your palms about two inches from each other. Feel them tingling? That's a manifestation of power. By rubbing your palms together and using the muscles in your arms and shoulders you're raising energy—magical power. It's flowing out from your palms as you hold them apart.

If you don't feel anything, practice this once or twice a day until you have success. Remember, don't force yourself to feel the power. Trying harder won't accomplish anything. Relax and *allow* yourself to feel what's been there all the time.

After you've actually sensed this energy, begin to fashion it into shapes. Use your visualization to do this. Directly after rubbing your hands, while they're still tingling, visualize jolts of energy—perhaps electric blue or purple—passing from your right (projective) palm to your left (receptive) palm. If you're left-handed, reverse the directions.*

Now envision this energy slowly swirling in a clockwise direction between your palms. Form it into a ball of glowing, pulsating, magical energy. See its dimensions, its colors. Feel its force and heat in your palms. This is a bit of energy that you've released from your body. There's nothing supernatural about it. Cup your hands around the ball. Make it grow or decrease in size *through your visualization*. Finally, push it into your stomach and absorb it back into your system.

This is not only great fun but is a valuable magical learning experience. When you've mastered the art of energy spheres, go on to feel energy fields.

Sit or stand before any plant. Herbs and plants in bloom seem to work best. In a pinch, cut flowers can be used as well. Breathe deeply for a few moments and clear your thoughts. Hold your receptive (left) palm a few inches above the plant. Pinpoint your consciousness to your palm. Do you feel a dull throbbing, a hum, a wave of heat, or simply a shift in the energies within your palm? Do you feel the inner force of the plant?

If so, good—you've felt energy. After you've accomplished this, try sensing the energies of stones and crystals.† Place a quartz crystal, say, on a table and pass your receptive hand over the crystal. Stretch out with your feelings and become aware of the nonvisible but viable energies that pulsate within the crystal.

---

* Remember the science fiction and fantasy movies you've seen wherein a magician sends power from his or her hands? Remember what it looked like in cinematic form? If you wish, use a similar image to visualize personal power streaming from your palms. Though that was just special effects, this, of course, is real, and we can use the picture to actually send out that power.

† For an indepth exercise in sensing stone energies see *Cunningham's Encyclopedia of Crystal, Gem & Metal Magic* (Llewellyn, 1988 and 2002).

All natural objects, remember, are manifestations of divine energy. With practice we can feel the power that resides within them.

If you have difficulty feeling these powers, rub your palms lightly together to sensitize them and try again.

This energy is the same power we're filled with when we're angry, nervous, terrified, joyous, or sexually aroused. It's the energy used in magic, whether we pull it from ourselves or channel it from the Goddess and God, plants, stones, and other objects. It is the stuff of creation that we utilize in magic.

Now that you've felt the power, use visualization to move it around. You needn't rub your palms together to raise energy—you can do this simply by concentrating on doing so. One of the easiest methods is to tighten up the muscles—tense your body. This raises energy, which is why we must relax in meditation. Meditation lowers our energy and allows us to drift from this world.

When you feel yourself bursting with power, hold out your right (projective) hand and direct energy from your body, through your arm, and out your fingers. Use your visualization. Really see and feel it streaming out.

For practice, stand in your home. Build the power within you. Direct it into each room, visualizing it sinking into the cracks and walls and around doors and windows. You're not creating a psychic burglar alarm but a magical protectant, so visualize the energy forming an impenetrable barrier across which no negativity or intruders can cross.

After "sealing" the house, halt the flow of energy. You can do this by visualizing it stopping and by shaking your hand. Sense your protective-powered energy resting within the walls. A secure, safe feeling should flood through you as you stand within your now guarded home.

Yes, you've done this with your mind, but also with power. Energy is real, and your ability to manipulate energy determines the effectiveness of your circles and rituals.

Work with feeling and directing the power daily. Make this a sort of magical play until you reach the point where you won't have to stop and think, "Can I do it? Can I raise the power?" You'll know you can.

12

Self-Dedication

IF YOU WISH to walk the Wiccan path, you may desire to dedicate yourself to the Goddess and God. This self-dedication is simply a formal ritual marking your conscious decision to embark on a new way of life—for that is the essence of Wicca.

At first I hesitated including a ritual of this sort here, feeling that the best dedicatory rituals were self-created. I've read and heard numerous stories of women and men who, drawn to Wicca but lacking access of covens or books, lit a candle, drank a little wine, and told the Gods of their intentions. That is perhaps the best sort of self-dedication ritual: simple and from the heart.

Many people feel more comfortable with formal rituals, however, so I'm including one at the end of this chapter. It is far different from most other such rites that have appeared in print, for it is an outdoor ritual that concentrates on contacting the energies of the Goddess and God.

This ritual is open to all who wish to use it. Before even considering dedicating yourself to the deities, however, be certain of your intentions for doing so, and that you have studied Wicca to the point where you know it is indeed the right way for you.

This means continued study. Read every book you can find on Wicca—the good ones as well as the bad. Subscribe to Wiccan and pagan publications. Familiarize yourself with Wicca as far as you can. Though some authors feel that their tradition is the only true one, don't let this stop you from reading their works. Similarly, don't accept everything you read simply because it appears in print.

In addition to reading, study nature. As you walk along the street, watch the birds flitting overhead, or bend down to gaze at an ant colony the way a mystic gazes into a crystal sphere. Celebrate the seasons and the phases of the moon with ritual.

You may also wish to fill your soul with music. If so, order by mail some of the Wiccan music tapes now available. (See appendix II, "Occult Suppliers.") If this is impossible, spend time each day listening to the music of nature—go to a place where wind blows through leaves or around tree trunks. Listen to water bubbling over stones or pounding a rocky coastline. Pinpoint your hearing to the meow of a lonely cat heralding the dawn. Create your own music too, if you are so talented.

Let your emotions be touched; whether by flute, recorder, and drum, or bird, river, and wind. Your decision to enter Wicca shouldn't be based solely on either your intellect or emotions; it should be a smooth product of both.

This done, stay up late a few nights or rise with the dawn. Alone, write down (even in the most broken sentences) what you hope to gain from Wicca. This may include spiritual fulfillment, deeper relationships with the Goddess and God, insight into your place in the world, the power to bring order into your existence, the ability to attune with the seasons and the earth, and so on.

Be specific, be ruthless, be complete. If you're not satisfied with this list, if it doesn't feel truthful, start over again. No one need ever see it. Copy down the final list in your mirror book, burn all other drafts, and be done with it.

Once this list has been fashioned, spend the next evening or morning creating a new one. On this, record what you feel you can give to Wicca.

This may surprise you, but every religion is the sum of its adherents. Unlike most orthodox religions, Wicca doesn't want your money, so don't write down "10 percent of my monthly income." This isn't because Wicca views money as debased or nonspiritual, but because money has been so abused and misused by most established religions. Wiccans don't live off Wicca.

Since Wicca doesn't condone proselytizing, has no leading figure, temples or central organizations, you may begin to wonder what you can do for Wicca. There is much you can give. Not only your time, energy, devotion, and so on, but also more concrete things. Here are some suggestions:

Join a national Wiccan or pagan group, such as the Pagan Spirit Alliance (through Circle—see appendix I). This helps you socialize with others of like mind, even if only through the mail or on the phone. Attend one of the public Wiccan or pagan gatherings held each year in various parts of the country.

Donate to an ecological organization, one striving to save our planet. Every day we poison the earth, as if we could spoil our camp and move elsewhere. If we don't take action now, there won't be anywhere to move. Financial contributions to responsible organizations dedicated to fighting pollution, saving endangered species, and bringing mindless development under control are examples of things you can give to Wicca.

The same goes for groups fighting to feed the hungry. Remember one fundamental idea—that which sustains life is sacred.

You may wish to start recycling. For many years, I've saved old newspapers, glass bottles, and aluminum cans from my trash. Since I live in a large city, there are numerous recycling centers nearby. Some centers pay, but the greatest rewards are not financial. They rest in the knowledge that we're helping to save the earth's natural resources.

If there are no recycling centers near you, be more conscious of your trash. Avoid purchasing products in plastic containers. Favor white paper products over colored ones—the dyes add to the pollution in our streams and rivers. Restrict or eliminate the use of plastic bags, food wrap, and other plastic products of the "use once, throw away" variety. These plastics don't break down (i.e., aren't biodegradable), are expensive, and may retain their same basic shapes for twenty-thousand years or more.

If you're reading this and asking yourself what this has to do with Wicca, set this book down, and put it away. Or, re-read it.

Wicca consists—in part—of *reverence for nature* as a manifestation of the Goddess and God. One way to reverence the earth is to care for her.

Following these suggestions, discover other ways to show your devotion to Wicca. A hint: anything you do for the earth, or for our fellow creatures on it, you do for Wicca.

The following self-dedication rite isn't designed to make you a Wicca—that comes with time and devotion (and not through initiation ceremonies). It is, in a mystical sense, a step toward linking your personal energies with those of the Goddess and God. It is a truly magical act which, if properly done, can change your life forever.

If you're hesitant, read this book again. You'll know when you're ready.

A Self-Dedication Rite

Prepare yourself by drawing a bath of warm water. Add a tablespoon or so of salt and a few drops of a scented oil such as sandalwood.

If you have no bath, use a shower. Fill a washcloth with salt, add a few drops of essential oil, and rub your body. If you're performing this ritual at the sea or a river, bathe there if you so desire.

As you bathe, prepare for the coming rite. Open your consciousness to higher levels of awareness. Deep breathe. Cleanse your mind as well as your body.

After bathing, dry and dress for the journey. Go to a place in the wild where you feel safe. It should be a comfortable spot where you won't be disturbed by others, an area where the powers of the earth and the elements are evident. It may be a mountain top, a desert canyon or cave, perhaps a dense forest, a rocky outcropping over the sea, a quiet island in the center of a lake. Even a lonely part of a park or garden can be used. Draw on your imagination to find the place.

You need take nothing with you but a vial of richly scented oil. Sandalwood, frankincense, cinnamon, or any other scent is fine. When you arrive at the place of dedication, remove your shoes and sit quietly for a few moments. Calm your heart if you've exerted yourself during your travel. Breathe deeply to return to normal, and keep your mind free of cluttered thoughts. Open yourself to the natural energies around you.

When you're calm, rise and pivot slowly on one foot, surveying the land around you. You're seeking the ideal spot. Don't try to find it; open your awareness to the place. When you've discovered it (and you'll know when), sit, kneel, or lie flat on your back. Place the oil on the earth beside you. Don't stand—contact the earth.

Continue deep breathing. Feel the energies around you. Call the Goddess and God in any words you like, or use the following invocation. Memorize these words before the rite so that they'll spill effortlessly from you, or improvise:

O Mother Goddess,
O Father God,
answers to all mysteries and yet mysteries unanswered;
in this place of power I open myself to your essence.
In this place and in this time I am changed;
from henceforth I walk the Wiccan path.
I dedicate myself to you, Mother Goddess and Father God.

(rest for moment, silent, still. Then continue:)

I breathe your energies into my body,
commingling, blending, mixing them with mine,
that I may see the divine in nature, nature in the divine,
and divinity within myself and all else.
O great Goddess, O great God,
make me one with your essence,
make me one with your essence,
make me one with your essence.

You may feel bursting with power and energy, or calm and at peace. Your mind might be in a whirl. The earth beneath you may throb and undulate with energy. Wild animals, attracted by the psychic occurrence, might grace you with their presence.

Whatever occurs, *know* that you have opened yourself and that the Goddess and God have heard you. You should feel different inside, at peace or simply powerful.

The Goddess   The God

Goddess and God symbols

After the invocation, wet a finger with the oil and mark these two symbols somewhere on your body (see above). It doesn't matter where; you can do this on your chest, forehead, arms, legs, anywhere. As you anoint, visualize these symbols sinking into your flesh, glowing as they enter your body, and then dispersing into millions of tiny points of light.

The formal self-dedication is ended. Thank the Goddess and God for their attention. Sit and meditate before leaving the place of dedication.

Once home, celebrate in some special way.

13

Ritual Design

Section III of this book contains a complete system of Wiccan rituals. I included this so that those without access to a Book of Shadows would have one, complete and ready for practical application and study.

This doesn't mean that these rituals are to be slavishly followed. This is not a tradition in the sense of something that has been handed down for years, but a viable example of a basic Wiccan Book of Shadows.

Since I want you to be free to write your own rituals, or to evolve them as the need arises, I decided that a chapter on ritual design was in order.

There's no great mystery concerning the structure of Wiccan rites, at least not anymore. Some say this is a good thing, this lessening of secrecy regarding Wicca. Others feel that it has stripped the religion of its romance. I understand this, but (as you well know by now) I also feel that Wicca should be available to all.

A chapter of this kind may seem harsh, focusing a rational, analytical light on spiritual matters. As my friend Barda once wrote to me, "Wicca is akin to a beautiful flower. If you rip off all its petals one by one to see how it's put together, you still have a flower, but it's not quite as beautiful." I hope to avoid this here.

First off, while I'm going to give you an overall structure for composing your own rituals, this structure isn't carved in stone. Most of the following nine points are basic to Wiccan rituals, although many use only some of them. They're an excellent guide to creating your own.

These are the nine basic components of Wiccan ritual:

1. Purification of self

2. Purification of space

3. Creating sacred space

4. Invocation

5. Ritual observance (on sabbats and esbats)

6. Energy raising (during magic)

7. Earthing the power

8. Thanking the Goddess and God

9. Breaking the circle

Purification of Self

This was covered in chapter 6, "Ritual and Preparation for Ritual." In essence, it consists of bathing, anointing your body with oil, meditation, deep breathing, and otherwise purifying your body, mind, and soul, and readying yourself for the coming rite.

This is truly a purification, an attempt to shrug off problems and thoughts of your everyday world. This is a time for calmness, for peace.

Although ritual bathing is common in Wicca, there are other methods of purifying the body. Stand in a rush of wind and visualize it carrying away negative thoughts and emotions.

Or use music: drumming softly for a few minutes is an excellent cleansing ritual (though your neighbors may have different views on it). Other instruments useful for purification include bells, gongs, sistrums (of the cleansing element of water) and guitars, violins, harps, and mandolins (instruments of the purifying element of fire).

This emphasis on purification shouldn't be taken out of context. Our bodies aren't breeding grounds for astral entities. We're exposed to negativity every day, however, from scenes of carnage and destruction in the papers and on the news and from our own dark thoughts. So these purifications aren't intended to chase away demons or devils; they simply free us of some of this negativity

While purifying yourself, remember to purify your thoughts as well. Prepare for the ritual. A Kahuna (an expert in the ancient Hawaiian system of magic, philosophy, religion, and applied technology*) once told me that the moment you think about performing a ritual *you are doing so.* It is already taking place. Energies are moving, consciousness is shifting.

During your ritual purification, know that you've already lit the candles, laid the circle, and invoked the Goddess and God. Don't think of the coming ritual, for it is already in progress.

This may seem a bit confusing, but it is an excellent tool to train your awareness.

Purification of Space

Outdoor ritual spaces rarely have to be purified. Indoor rituals, though, usually require it. Most living spaces accumulate "astral garbage," pockets of negativity and other energies that collect in human habitations. Since these energies can be disruptive, the area is ritually cleansed prior to actual workings.

There are two specifics here: indoor and outdoor rituals.

For in-home rites, if you're alone in the house, lock the door, take the phone off the hook, and close the curtains. You must be assured of absolute privacy and lack of interruptions during the ritual. If others are home, tell them you're not to be disturbed until further notice.

If this presents a problem and a mate or your family won't give you any time to yourself, work your rituals late at night or early in the morning when others are asleep.

Clean the floor physically. Sweep with a regular broom, vacuum, or mop. Once clean, it can be purified with the old Witch's tool, the magic broom.

---

* Such as canoe building, navigation, and medicinal herbalism.

You needn't actually touch the bristles to the floor. Do, however, brush briskly, visualizing the broom sweeping away negativity, ill, and psychic clutter. You might visualize the broom shooting out sparks, or perhaps flaming with an intense blue or violet light that burns negativity to ashes. Visualize and know that the broom is magically cleansing the room. It will be so.

Another way to purify the ritual area is to scatter salt, either alone or mixed with a powdered herb or resin such as thyme, rosemary, frankincense, copal, sage, or dragon's blood.* Salt water is also used. The scattering action releases the energies resident within the salt and herbs and these, directed and magnified by your ritual intent and visualization, drive away the disturbing energies. *Do this with power.*

Or, play a musical instrument to the four quarters while walking clockwise around the area. In general, ascending scales purify. You might also chant, especially sounds that you feel set up protective and purifying energies. You can discover these through experimentation and heightened psychic awareness.

You can also simply burn an herb with proven "clearing" qualities as an incense, such as frankincense, myrrh, sage, thyme, or rosemary, alone or in combination. Fumigate the ritual space with the smoke and visualize it driving away negativity.

Outdoor rituals require a minimum of cleansing. Most of the natural environment is far less psychically polluted than are our homes and other buildings. A traditional light sweeping with the magic broom (in this case, to actually brush away fallen leaves or pebbles as well as negativity), backed up with your visualization, will suffice. Sprinkling pure water is also fine but, since salt can be harmful to plants, it's best not to use it outdoors.

---

* Before using any herb for magical purposes, hold it in your hands and, while visualizing, infuse it with your programmed, personal power. This increases its effectiveness.

Creating Sacred Space

This section consists of arranging the altar (if it isn't a permanent one) and forming the magic circle. In chapter 7, "The Magic Circle" and the Altar, I discussed these topics at length, and so will limit my comments here to a few.

Though many Wiccans place their altars in the center of the area, and indeed in the center of the future magic circle, others do not. Some place it in one of the "corners" of the circle, next to its edge, usually in the north or east. This, they say, makes it easier to move around the circle. I find it to be exactly the opposite. Additionally, it restricts your possible methods of forming the circle.

It doesn't matter which you use, so try both and find out which works the best for you.

I use two altars. One's permanent, the other is erected only for rituals. I always place the altar in the center of the circle, facing north, if only because this is familiar to me. Besides, if I put it at the northern edge of the circle, I'd probably kick it over.

Now to the circle, or "sphere of power." You'll find one form of circle casting in *The Standing Stones Book of Shadows.* There are many other types, and indeed that particular form can't be used in every situation. One of these variants may be more to your liking (or better suited to your ritual space).

The first is more heavily dependent upon your visualization and magical abilities than others, for it uses no tools but your mind.

To help your visualization, place a purple cord or some other object(s) on the ground to mark the circle's circumference. Stand before the altar, or in the center of the circle (during outdoor rituals you might not have an altar). Face east or the preferred direction. Build the power within you. When it has reached a fine pitch (you'll know with practice), hold your projective hand palm down, waist level. Point your fingers toward the edge of the future circle.

See and *feel* the energy flowing out from your fingertips in a stream of vibrating purplish-blue light. Slowly walk the circle, clockwise. Push the power out and form it with your visualization into a circling band of glowing magical light, the exact width of your circle (usually nine feet or less). This circle should hang around you and the altar.

When this band of light is swirling in the air, stretch it with your visualization. See it expanding and increasing in size. Form it into a dome of energy surrounding the ritual area. It should touch the earth precisely aligned with your cord ring, if any. Now extend this energy down into the earth until it forms a complete sphere as you stand in its center.

The circle should be a living, glowing reality. Feel its energy. Sense the edge of the circle. Sense the difference in vibration within and without it. Contrary to popular Wiccan teachings, pushing your hand into or walking through a magic sphere will cause no astral damage, any more than will walking through a protective power shield set up around your home. After all, most magic circles are so designed that if you stand near the circle's edge, your head and half your torso extend outside it. Walking through the circle, at most, will give you a jolt of energy. It will also dissipate it. If this happens, simply form it again.

When the circle seems complete and solid around you, break off the flow of energy from your projective hand by turning your palm downward and pulling it back to your body. Shut off the flow. Shake your hand if necessary to break it.

Next, you may wish to invoke the rulers of the four quarters of the circle. There are varied Wiccan teachings and ideas regarding these four rulers. Some link them with the elements; thus the "spirit" or ruler of the east is related to air; the south, to fire; the west, to water; the north, to earth.

Then again, some Wiccans don't see them as necessarily elemental in nature, but simply as anciently placed guardians or watchers of the four directions, perhaps created by the goddesses and gods of earlier times.

Still other Wiccans view them as the Mighty Ones, former humans who have spiraled up the incarnational path until they've reached perfection. This allows them to "dwell with the Goddess and God." These Mighty Ones are mythologically linked to the four directions.

Perhaps it's best to get in touch with these energies and discover them for yourself. No matter how you view these rulers, open yourself to them during invocation. Don't just say the words or visualize the colors during the circle casting; invite them to be present. Stretch out with your awareness. *Know* whether they've arrived or not.

Too many Wiccans say the words but don't check their effectiveness. The words are the least important part of a Wiccan ritual, save for their use in promoting ritual consciousness.

Words don't have to be used to invoke the rulers, but they're tools that train the attention, focus our awareness, and stir up the emotions—when properly stated. You can use the invocations in the circle casting section of the book or write your own.

To leave the circle during a ritual, cut a doorway (see section III). This preserves the flow of energy around the circle save for a small section that you clear. Through this you can pass to the outside world without unduly disturbing the rest of the circle. Just remember to close it after returning.

Another, simpler form of circle construction uses physical activity to raise power, and is easier to do if you're not quite fluent with energy raising. Stand facing north at the edge of the future circle. Turn to the right and walk slowly, marking out the circle's edge with your feet.*

As you continue your ritual tread, you may wish to chant Goddess or God names, or perhaps both. You might think of their presence or simply shift your awareness to the energy that your body is generating. If you've placed the altar to one side of the circle, move a few feet inward as you pass by it.

Continue to move clockwise, but gently increase your pace. The energy will slide off your body and, picked up by your momentum, will be carried around with you in your circular path.

Move faster. Feel the energy flowing within you. You may feel a sensation such as you feel when walking in water—the energy will move with you as you release it. Sense your personal power creating a

---

* In the Northern Hemisphere, most Wiccans move clockwise within the circle, except during some banishing rituals. In Australia and in other parts of the Southern Hemisphere, circles may be cast counterclockwise, as this is the apparent direction in which the sun moves.

sphere of energy around the altar. When this is firmly established, invoke the four quarters and the rites can begin.

Both of the above methods are ideal for rituals wherein magic will take place, but for purely religious rites such constructions of psychic energy are not strictly necessary. Though the circle is thought of as being "between the worlds," and a meeting place with the Goddess and God, we needn't create such psychic temples to commune with the deities of nature, nor do they appear when called like pets. Wiccan ritual is used to expand our awareness of them, not the other way around.

Therefore, complex circle castings (such as the one in section III) aren't always necessary, especially during outdoor rites where such circles are usually impossible to construct. Fortunately, there are simpler forms that can be used.

An outdoor circle casting may entail nothing more than placing a stick of burning incense at each of the quarters. Start in the north and move clockwise around the circle. Invoke the quarters.

A circle can also be traced in the sand or dirt with a finger, a wand, or the white-handled knife. This is ideal for sea and forest rituals.

Or, you may wish to place objects to mark out the circle's perimeter. Vegetation is particularly appropriate: flowers for spring, pine and holly for winter (see "An Herbal Grimoire" in *The Standing Stones Book of Shadows* for other suggestions). A ring of small river-polished stones or quartz crystals are other possibilities.

Some Wiccans pour a small, unbroken circle of some substance to define the ritual space. Powdered herbs, flour (as was used in ancient Middle Eastern rituals as well as in contemporary Voodoo rites), crushed colored minerals, sand, or salt are poured out while moving clockwise. As mentioned above, a cord can also be laid in a ring.

For more information regarding circle construction, see *The Standing Stones Book of Shadows*.

Invocation

In some ways this is the heart of all Wiccan ritual, and indeed is the only necessary part. Wiccan rites are attunements with the powers that are the Goddess and God; all else is pageantry.*

The word "invocation" shouldn't be taken too literally. This usually refers to a spoken prayer or verse, but may also consist of music, dance, gestures, and song.

There are several invocations to the Goddess and God in *The Standing Stones Book of Shadows*. Feel free to use them when designing your own rituals, but remember that impromptu invocations are often more effective than the most ancient prayers.

If you do write up your own invocations, you may wish to incorporate a rhyme. Centuries of magical tradition attest to the value of rhyme. It certainly makes invocations that much easier to memorize.

Rhyme also contacts the unconscious or psychic mind. It drowses our societally, materially, and intellectually based minds and lets us slip into ritual consciousness.

When actually invoking, don't curse if you forget a word, mispronounce something, or entirely lose your train of thought. This is quite natural and is usually a manifestation of fatigue, stress, or a desire to be word perfect in the circle.

Invocation requires a willingness to open yourself to the Goddess and God. It needn't be a pristine performance. As most rituals begin with invocation, this is, in a sense, the moment of truth. If the invocation isn't sincere, it won't contact the Goddess and God within, and the ritual that follows will be nothing more than form.

Practice invoking the Goddess and God, not only in ritual but daily, throughout your life. Remember: Wiccan practice isn't limited to full moons or sabbats—it is a round-the-clock way of life.

---

* Though it should, of course, promote ritual consciousness. Outdoor rituals rarely need as much invocation because the Wiccans are already surrounded by natural manifestations of the deities.

In a more metaphysical sense, invocation is a dual-level act. It not only invokes the Goddess and God, it also awakens us (shifts our awareness) to that part of us that is divine—our inviolable, intransmutable essence: our link with the Old Ones.

In other words, when you invoke do so not only to higher forces but also to the deities that dwell within, to that spark of divine energy that exists inside all living creatures.

The powers behind all deities are one. They are resident within all humans. This explains why all religions merge at their cores, and why they work for their respective adherents. If only one correct way of approaching deity were possible, there would be one religious ideal. This will never happen.

The concept of the Goddess and God dwelling within may seem egotistical (we're all divine!) but only from an unbalanced viewpoint. Yes, when some people grasp this idea they start acting as if they were indeed divine. Seeing the divinity within all other humans helps bring this idea into balance.

While we are, in a sense, immortal (our souls certainly are), we are not the Immortal Ones. We're not the universal, timeless, transcendent beings that are revered in all religions.

Call the Goddess and God with love and sincerity, and your rituals should be blessedly successful.

Ritual Observance

This usually follows the invocation, if the ritual is held on a sabbat or esbat. It may also be a rite of meditation, transition, thanksgiving, or simply a few moments to commune. In such cases, ritual observances may or may not be appropriate.

You needn't be glum, serious, or stodgy while doing these rituals. Wiccans are serious about their religion, but that doesn't mean that the deities are.* Laughter has its ritual and magical functions. For example,

---

* Most Wiccans have favorite stories of circle mishaps. One of mine occurred when leading a ritual. I mispronounced the name of the elemental ruler of earth ("Goob" rather than "Ghob"); the double-headed axe fell to the floor from the altar, and I smacked my hands into the chandelier that hung over the altar during power raising. It was a funny ritual.

truly laughing at a curse can destroy its effects. It sets up a powerful protective energy surrounding you through which no negative energies can penetrate. Laughter releases tremendous amounts of personal power.

So when you spill the salt, tip over a candle, fail to light the incense, and forget the verse, laugh and start over. Too many newcomers to Wicca bring their ideas of stern, solemn religion with them into the magic circle, but these ideas are alien to Wicca.

Leave those thoughts behind you. Wicca is a religion of peace and happiness and yes, even laughter. Wiccan ritual needs no pomposity unless it is simply desired.

Energy Raising

In practice, this is magic—the movement of natural energies to effect needed change. You can raise energy at most Wiccan rituals, though it is rarely thought to be mandatory. The full moons, solstices, and equinoxes, however, are classic times to perform magic, for there are extra earth energies afoot that can be utilized to enhance the effectiveness of your magic.

This doesn't mean that Wiccan rituals are simply excuses to work magic. Though it is perfectly permissible to work magic on the eight days of power (indeed, it is traditional), many Wiccans don't, preferring these to be times of attunement and celebration rather than of magic.

One of the major differences, however, between Wicca and most other religions is its acceptance of magic, not just in the hands of specialized priests who work miracles while others watch, but to all who practice its rituals. Therefore, magic can be worked with a clear conscience at most Wiccan rituals after invocation and ritual observance.

In magic, ensure that your need is real, that you're emotionally involved in this need, and that you know that your magic will work. Some of the simplest spells are the most effective. After all these years I often prefer to use colored candles, oils, and herbs as focal points of energy. There are countless ways to practice magic; find one that's right for you (see bibliography for related books).

As I've written elsewhere, magic is magic. It isn't religious in the usual sense of the word. In Wicca, however, magic is usually worked while invoking the Goddess and God, asking for their presence, and that they lend their strength to the task. It is this that makes Wiccan magic religious.

The magic circle (or sphere) is formed to retain power during energy raising. When building up power for a spell in one of the old ways (dance, endless chanting, visualization, and so on), Wiccans attempt to hold it inside their bodies until it has reached its peak. At this time it is released and sent toward its goal. It is difficult to retain all of this power—especially during dance—and so the circle does this job. Once you've released the power, however, the circle in no way impedes the flow of energy to its destination.

Circles aren't necessary for the practice of magic, though if you invoke the Goddess and God to help you, the presence of the circle ensures that the power you receive will be properly retained until you decide it's time to send it forth.

Ask the Goddess and God to assist you, to grant your request or to amplify your own powers, no matter what type of magic you perform in the circle.* In doing so you're expanding your awareness of the deities within, opening a channel through which divine energy can flow. Thank the Goddess and God after the finished ritual in words, by lighting a candle, or by leaving an offering of food or drink on an offering plate or in the ground.

Few words should be required here regarding "evil" magic. Needless to say, any magic that is designed to harm or control another living being—even if you feel that it's in their best interest—is negative magic. This leaves you open to receiving negativity back. Negative magic isn't Wiccan magic.

Once you've finished your magical working, pause for a few moments. Gaze at the Goddess and God candles or at their images on the altar. You might also look at the rising incense smoke or bowl of fresh flowers.

---

* As long as it is positive.

Think of the deities and of your relationship with them, as well as your place in the universe. Put all thoughts of the ritual out of your mind entirely by shifting your awareness away from it.

You'll probably be drained of energy if you did indeed release power, so sink back down and relax for a few moments. This is a reflective moment. It smoothly flows into the next ritual step.

Earthing the Power

Once you've sent energy, residual power usually rushes around within you. Some traces may still exist inside the circle. This should be earthed, or reprogrammed to fit smoothly back within your normal energy scheme. Even if you've performed no magic, an earthing is desirable before closing down the ritual, for this step, especially when it consists of a meal, has sacred aspects as well.

Some Wiccans call this Cakes and Wine or Cakes and Ale. In *The Standing Stones Book of Shadows* I've termed it The Simple Feast. It's all the same thing—a ritual ingestion of food and drink to ease us back from ecstasy.

Eating kicks your body into a different mode. Since food is a product of the earth, it gently returns our awareness to the physical reality. Food is a manifestation of divine energy. Eating is a form of true communion.

This meal can be a light snack of cookies and milk, juice and bread, cheese and wine, perhaps the traditional crescent-shaped cakes (actually cookies) and wine (see "Recipes"—in *The Standing Stones Book of Shadows*) are all fine. The food is often blessed prior to eating, and you'll find sample rituals for this in *The Standing Stones Book of Shadows*.

Prior to eating, make a small offering to the Goddess and God by scattering cake crumbs and pouring a few drops of liquid onto the ground. If indoors, place these things in a special libation bowl. Bury its contents in the ground outside as soon as possible after the ritual.

There are other methods of earthing yourself and the power.

Tasting a bit of salt and scattering it around the circle works. You might also try visualization. See the excess energy as a kind of purplish mist hanging in the circle and within yourself. Hold up a tool of some kind (the magic knife, a rock, the pentacle, or something else) and visualize it absorbing the extra energy. (Try holding this with your receptive hand as well.) When the circle is cleared and you feel back to normal, put down the tool. When doing this with your magic knife (athame), the extra energy can later be used for spells and for forming the magic circle. There are many possibilities; some Wiccans store candles beneath the altar and send the excess energy into them.

Thanking the Gods

The next phase of Wiccan ritual consists of thanking the Goddess and God for their presence and attendance at your circle. This can be done in specific ways, with gestures or chants or music, or can be improvised on the spot.

Some Wiccans think of this as dismissing the deities. I shudder at the very notion. Imagine some puny little Wiccan telling the Goddess and God that they can leave!*

Thank them for their attention and ask that they come again. That's it.

Breaking the Circle

The method in which you return an area or room to its normal state depends on your method of circle casting. If you use the one in *The Standing Stones Book of Shadows*, close with the accompanying ritual. In this section we'll look at the methods to disperse the circles described in "Creating Sacred Space" above.

The first one, in which the circle is visualized as swirling around you and the altar, is the easiest. Thank the rulers for attending the rite. Stand before the altar again. Hold out your receptive hand (it will be the right if you're left-handed). Visualize yourself absorbing the energy that created the circle. Feel the energy sinking back into your palm and, thusly, into your body.

---

* Besides, they never leave. They exist within ourselves and inside all of nature.

You can also use the magical knife to "cut" the circle. Visualize its power surging back into the blade and handle.

The next method is one to which some Wiccans take offense, but it is based on orthodox Wiccan teachings. If you created your circle by treading clockwise around the altar, stand in the north and move slowly to the west, the south, and the east, ending back in the north again. As you move, draw the energy from the circle within yourself.*

For other types of circles, "break" or disperse them in some way. If you laid stones in a ring around the altar, take them up. Remove flowers or greens if they mark the circle's perimeter and disperse or sweep up rings of herbs, salt, or flour.

Whatever method you use, thank the rulers of the four quarters for their presence and ask that they watch over future rites.

When the circle is gone, put away the ritual tools. If you've used salt and water (as in the circle consecration in *The Standing Stones Book of Shadows*), save the excess salt for future use, but pour the water onto the bare earth. Offerings in the libation bowl should be buried along with the incense ashes, though these last are sometimes saved for future spells and rites.

It isn't necessary to immediately take down the altar. Indeed, it can be left for the rest of the night or day. When you do begin putting the tools away, it's good symbolism to wait to quench the candles until last. Use a snuffer, your fingers or your white-handled knife blade (clean off the wax and soot after each use). Start with the quarter candles and any others that you might have used, then put out the God taper and finally the Goddess candle.

Your rite has ended.

---

* Those south of the equator would perform this and all circle dispersions in exactly the opposite direction. Some Wiccans believe that any counterclockwise (widdershins) movement is negative, but it is used here for a sound reason and, indeed, this is the way the circle is broken in at least one Wiccan tradition that I know of. If you feel uncomfortable when treading widdershins, simply walk clockwise and take the energy back inside you.

Section III

The Standing Stones
Book of Shadows

Introduction to
The Standing Stones
Book of Shadows

THIS IS A COMPLETE Book of Shadows, ready for use. I wrote much of it several years ago for students who desired to practice Wicca but couldn't gain entrance to a coven. There is certainly nothing secret here, nor am I borrowing from other traditions except in the most general ways.

I'm limiting my remarks, notes, and comments on this Book of Shadows. If you have questions while reading these rituals, or while working them, settle them as best you can. Unfamiliar words and terms can be checked in the glossary.

Please remember that this is simply *one* Book of Shadows. There are countless others, each with both strong and weak points. Some of these have been printed, in part or in their entirety (see bibliography).

This is not, I repeat, *not* sacred writ, nor does it consist of revealed writings. I've written it in a somewhat romantic, baroque style, hoping that this will spark your imagination. Remember, the Book of Shadows isn't changeless. Feel free to alter anything for any reason, or use this Book of Shadows as a pattern to construct your own. It isn't my intention to begin a new tradition of Wicca.

The rites are constructed for individuals. Group workings will require some alterations.

Why the "standing stones?" I've long been fascinated by the megalithic sites of Britain and Europe. Stone circles and menhirs capture my imagination, and I wonder what rites their ancient creators performed there.*

---

* These weren't the Druids; Druids arrived over a thousand years later and had nothing to do with the construction of such sites as Stonehenge. Sorry!

I centered this system's circle casting around the erection of a psychic circle of stones, as well as a physical one. If you feel uncomfortable with this idea, simply change the ritual. Never be afraid to do this—you won't disappear into a poof of dust. No angry deities will descend unless you use rites calling for blood or death or living sacrifices, or perform magic that harms or twists others to your will.

While working these or any other rituals, remember to visualize, sense, and move power. Feel the presence of the Goddess and God. If you don't, all rituals are only form.

It is my hope that this Book of Shadows captures your imagination and guides you on the Wiccan path.

For those who are interested, the way is open.

Blessed Be!

Words to the Wise

O DAUGHTERS AND sons of the earth, adore the Goddess and God and be blessed with the fullness of life.

Know that they have brought you to these writings, for herein lie our ways of Wicca, to serve and fulfill the keepers of wisdom, the tenders of the sacred flame of knowledge. Run the rites with love and joy, and the Goddess and God will bless you with all that you need. But those who practice dark magics shall know their greatest wrath.

Remember that you are of the Wicca. No more do you trod the ways of doubt. You walk the path of light, ever climbing from shadow to shadow to the highest realm of existence. But though we're the bearers of truths, others do not wish to share our knowledge, so we run our rites beneath moon-filled skies enwrapped in shadows. But we are happy.

Live fully, for that is the purpose of life. Refrain not from earthly existence. From it we grow to learn and understand, until such time that we are reborn to learn more, repeating this cycle 'till we have spiraled up the path of perfection and can finally call the Goddess and God our kin.

Walk the fields and forests; be refreshed by the cool winds and the touch of a nodding flower. The moon and sun sing in the ancient wild places: the deserted seashore, the stark desert, the roaring waterfall. We are of the earth and should revere her, so do her honor.

Celebrate the rites on the appropriate days and seasons, and call upon the Goddess and God when the time is meet, but use the Power only when necessary, never for frivolous ends. Know that using the Power for harm is a perversion of life itself.

But for those who love and magnify love, the richness of life shall be your reward. Nature will celebrate.

So love the Goddess and God, and harm none!

The Nature of Our Way

As often as possible, hold the rites in forests, by the seashore, on deserted mountaintops, or near tranquil lakes. If this is impossible, a garden or some chamber shall suffice, if it is readied with fumes or flowers.

Seek out wisdom in books, rare manuscripts, and cryptic poems if you will, but seek it out also in simple stones, and fragile herbs, and in the cries of wild birds. Listen to the whisperings of the wind and the roar of water if you would discover magic, for it is here that the old secrets are preserved.

Books contain words; trees contain energies and wisdom books ne'er dreamt of.

Ever remember that the Old Ways are constantly revealing themselves. Therefore be as the river willow that bends and sways with the wind. That which remains changeless shall outlive its spirit, but that which evolves and grows will shine for centuries.

There can be no monopoly on wisdom. Therefore share what you will of our ways with others who seek them, but hide mystic lore from the eyes of those who would destroy, for to do otherwise increases their destruction.

Mock not the rituals or spells of another, for who can say yours are greater in power or wisdom?

Ensure that your actions are honorable, for all that you do shall return to you three-fold, good or bane.

Be wary of one who would dominate you, who would control and manipulate your workings and reverences. True reverence for the Goddess and God occurs within. Look with suspicion on any who would twist worship from you for their own gain and glory, but welcome those priestesses and priests who are suffused with love.

Honor all living things, for we are of the bird, the fish, the bee.
Destroy not life save it be to preserve your own.

And this is the nature of our way.

Before Time Was

Before time was, there was The One; The One was all, and all was The One.

And the vast expanse known as the universe was The One, all wise, all-pervading, all-powerful, eternally changing.

And space moved. The One molded energy into twin forms, equal but opposite, fashioning the Goddess and God from The One and of The One.

The Goddess and God stretched and gave thanks to The One, but darkness surrounded them. They were alone, solitary save for The One.

So they formed energy into gasses and gasses into suns and planets and moons; they sprinkled the universe with whirling globes and so all was given shape by the hands of the Goddess and God.

Light arose and the sky was illuminated by a billion suns. And the Goddess and God, satisfied by their works, rejoiced and loved, and were one.

From their union sprang the seeds of all life, and of the human race, so that we might achieve incarnation upon the earth.

The Goddess chose the moon as her symbol, and the God the sun as his symbol, to remind the inhabitants of earth of their fashioners.

All are born, live, die, and are reborn beneath the sun and moon; all things come to pass there under, and all occurs with the blessings of The One, as has been the way of existence before time was.

Song of the Goddess
(based on an invocation by Morgan*)

I am the Great Mother,
worshipped by all creation and existent prior to their consciousness.
I am the primal female force, boundless and eternal.

I am the chaste Goddess of the moon, the lady of all magic.
The winds and moving leaves sing my name.
I wear the crescent moon upon my brow
and my feet rest among the starry heavens.
I am mysteries yet unsolved, a path newly set upon.
I am a field untouched by the plow.
Rejoice in me and know the fullness of youth.

I am the blessed Mother, the gracious lady of the harvest.
I am clothed with the deep, cool wonder of the earth
and the gold of the fields heavy with grain.
By me the tides of the earth are ruled;
all things come to fruition according to my season.
I am refuge and healing.
I am the life-giving Mother, wondrously fertile.

Worship me as the crone,
tender of the unbroken cycle of death and rebirth.
I am the wheel, the shadow of the moon.
I rule the tides of women and men and
give release and renewal to weary souls.
Though the darkness of death is my domain,
the joy of birth is my gift.

---

* My first teacher and priestess. This and the following "Call of the God" aren't necessarily meant to be spoken in ritual. They can be read for devotional purposes, meditated upon to learn more of the Goddess and God, or used in ritual by inserting the words "she" and "he" and making other small changes to agree with these alterations.

I am the Goddess of the moon, the earth, the seas.
My names and strengths are manifold.
I pour forth magic and power, peace and wisdom.
I am the eternal maiden, Mother of all, and crone of darkness,
and I send you blessings of limitless love.

Call of the God

I am the radiant king of the heavens,
flooding the earth with warmth and
encouraging the hidden seed of creation
to burst forth into manifestation.
I lift my shining spear to light the lives of all beings and
daily pour forth my gold upon the earth,
putting to flight the powers of darkness.

I am the master of the beasts wild and free.
I run with the swift stag and
soar as a sacred falcon against the shimmering sky.
The ancient woods and wild places emanate my powers,
and the birds of the air sing of my sanctity.

I am also the last harvest,
offering up grain and fruits beneath the sickle of time
so that all may be nourished.
For without planting there can be no harvest;
without winter, no spring.

Worship me as the thousand-named sun of creation,
the spirit of the horned stag in the wild, the endless harvest.
See in the yearly cycle of festivals my birth, death, and rebirth—
and know that such is the destiny of all creation.

I am the spark of life, the radiant sun,
the giver of peace and rest,
and I send my rays of blessings to warm the hearts
and strengthen the minds of all.

The Circle of Stones

The circle of stones is used during indoor rituals, for energy raising, meditation, and so on.

First, cleanse the area with the ritual broom.

For this circle you will need four large, flat stones. If you have none, candles can be used to mark the four cardinal points of the circle. White or purple candles can be used, as can colors related to each direction—green for the north, yellow for east, red for south, and blue for west.

Place the first stone (or candle) to the north, to represent the spirit of the north stone. In ritual when you invoke the spirits of the stones you're actually invoking all that resides in that particular direction, including the elemental energies.

After setting the north stone (or candle), place the east, south and west stones. They should mark out a rough square, nearly encompassing the working area. This square represents the physical plane on which we exist—the earth.

Now take a long purple or white cord* and lay it out in a circle, using the four stones or candles to guide you. It takes a bit of practice to smoothly do this. The cord should be placed so that the stones remain inside the circle. Now you have a square and a circle, the circle representing the spiritual reality. As such, this is a squared circle; the place of interpenetration of the physical and spiritual realms.

The size of the circle can be anything from five to twenty feet depending on the room and your desires.

Next, set up the altar. The following tools are recommended:

- A Goddess symbol (candle, holed stone, statue)
- A God symbol (candle, horn, acorn, statue)
- Magic knife (athame)
- Wand
- Censer

---

* Fashioned, perhaps, of braided yarn.

Goddess symbol or candle	Censer	God symbol or candle
Bowl of water		Bowl of salt
	Red candle	
Cup		Incense
	Pentacle	
Crystal		
		Knife/wand
	Cauldron or spell materials	
Bell		Bolline

Suggested altar layout

- Pentacle
- A bowl of water (spring, rain, or tap)
- A bowl of salt (it can also be placed on the pentacle)
- Incense
- Flowers and greens
- One red candle in holder (if not using point candles)
- Any other tools or materials required for the ritual, spell, or magical working

Set up the altar according to the plan shown here or according to your own design. Also, be sure to have plenty of matches, as well as a small heat-proof container in which to place them when used. A charcoal block is also necessary to burn the incense.

Light the candles. Set the incense smoking. Lift the knife and touch its blade to the water, saying:

> *I consecrate and cleanse this water*
> *that it may be purified and fit to*
> *dwell within the sacred circle of stones.*
> *In the name of the Mother Goddess and the Father God**
> *I consecrate this water.*

As you do this, visualize your knife blasting away all negativity from the water.

The salt is next touched with the point of the knife while saying:

> *I bless this salt that it may be fit*
> *to dwell within the sacred circle of stones.*
> *In the name of the Mother Goddess and the Father God,*
> *I bless this salt.*

Now stand facing north, at the edge of the cord-marked circle. Hold your magic knife point outward at waist level. Walk slowly around the circle's perimeter clockwise, your feet just inside the cord, charging it with your words and energy. Create the circle—through your visualization—with the power flowing out from your knife's blade. As you walk, stretch the energy out until it forms a complete sphere around the working area, half above the ground, half below. As you do this say:

> *Here is the boundary of the circle of stones.*
> *Naught but love shall enter in,*
> *naught but love shall emerge from within.*
> *Charge this by your powers, Old Ones!*

When you have arrived back at the north, place the magic knife on the altar. Take up the salt and sprinkle it around the circle, beginning and ending in the north, and moving clockwise. Next, carry the smoking censer around the circle, then the southern point candle or the lit red candle from the altar, and finally sprinkle water around the circle. Do more than carrying and walking, sense the substances purifying the circle. The circle of stones is now sealed.

---

* If you are attuning with a specific goddess and god, substitute their names here.

Hold aloft the wand at the north, at the edge of the circle, and say:

> *O spirit of the north stone,*
> *ancient one of the earth,*
> *I call you to attend this circle.*
> *Charge this by your powers, Old Ones!*

As you say this, visualize a greenish mist rising and writhing in the northern quarter, over the stone. This is the elemental energy of earth. When the spirit is present, lower the wand, move to the east, raise it again, and say:

> *O spirit of the east stone,*
> *ancient one of air,*
> *I call you to attend this circle.*
> *Charge this by your powers, Old Ones!*

Visualize the yellowish mist of air energy. Lower the wand, move to the south and repeat the following with your upraised wand, visualizing a crimson fire mist:

> *O spirit of the south stone,*
> *ancient one of fire,*
> *I call you to attend this circle.*
> *Charge this by your powers, Old Ones!*

Finally, to the west, say with wand held aloft:

> *O spirit of the west stone,*
> *ancient one of water,*
> *I call you to attend this circle.*
> *Charge this by your powers, Old Ones!*

Visualize the bluish mist, the essence of water.

The circle breathes and lives around you. The spirits of the stones are present. Feel the energies. Visualize the circle glowing and growing in power. Stand still, sensing for a moment.

The circle of stones is complete. The Goddess and God may be called, and magic wrought.

Cutting a Doorway

At times you may have to leave the circle. This is fine, of course, but as previously mentioned, passing through the circle dissipates it. To prevent this from occurring, it's traditional to cut a doorway.

To do this, face northeast. Hold your magic knife point downward near the ground. *See* and *sense* the circle before you. Pierce its wall of energy with the athame and trace an archway, tall enough to walk through, moving counterclockwise along the circle for about three feet. Move the point of the magic knife up at the arch's center and down the other side until it is near the ground.

As you're doing this, visualize that area of the circle's energy being sucked back into the athame. This creates a void, allowing passage in and out of the circle. Pull the magic knife out of the circle's wall. You're free to walk outside.

Once back inside, close the door by placing the athame at the lower northeastern* point of the archway. With your knife, trace the circle's perimeter clockwise, as if redrawing that portion of the circle of stones, again visualizing blue or purple energy flaring out from the blade and converging with the rest of the circle. It is done.

Releasing the Circle

Once the rite is ended, face north, hold aloft the wand and say:

> *Farewell, spirit of the north stone.*
> *I give thanks for your presence here.*
> *Go in power.*

Repeat this same formula to the east, south, and west, substituting the proper direction in the words. Then return to the north and hold the wand aloft for a few moments.

---

* The traditional direction. In some covens, members enter and withdraw from the circle from this point.

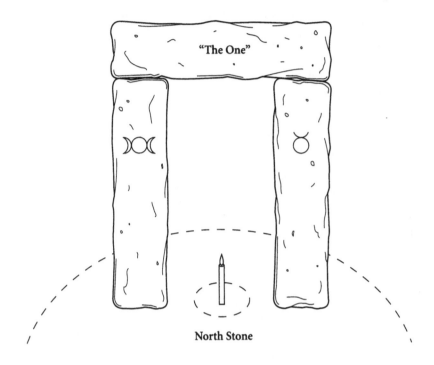

North Stone

North trilithon visualization

Lay the wand on the altar. Take up the athame. Standing in the north, pierce the circle's wall with the blade at waist level. Move clockwise around the circle, visualizing its power being sucked back into the knife. Literally pull it back into the blade and handle. Sense the circle dissolving, shrinking, the outside world slowly regaining its dominance in the area.

When you arrive at the north again, the circle is no more.

Visualizations for the Circle of Stone

If you wish, you can back up the circle casting with the following visualizations as you form the circle itself:

Prepare as usual. Approach the north and set the north stone (or the candle) on the ground. Then, visualize a stone slab standing upright two feet to the left of and behind the north stone. Visualize this as being bluish-gray, two-feet wide, two-feet thick, and six-feet tall. This stone represents the Goddess (see figure on previous page).

When the stone is really there—in your visualization—create another stone of the same size and color two feet to the right of the north stone. This represents the God.

Now visualize a capstone resting on top of the two upright stones. It is about two feet by two feet by five feet. This represents The One before the Goddess and God, the source of all power and magic. The northern trilithon is now complete.

The stones form an archway, a symbol of and gateway to the realm of the element of earth.

Firmly visualize this, then gaze through the arch formed by the stones. See the greenish haze of earth energy.

Repeat the entire procedure to the east, south, and west. Visualize the appropriate elemental color within each trilithon.

Now purify salt and water, cast the circle as usual, and carry around the salt, censer, candle, and water.

As you approach each quarter to call its spirit of the stone, see the trilithon firmly in your mind. Visualize it in all its pagan splendor. See the elemental hazes within them, boiling and writhing in unmanifestedness. Stretch out with your feelings; sense the arrival of the spirit of each stone, then go on to the next.

With practice this comes easily, but such visualizations are never necessary.

The Blessing Chant

May the powers of The One,
the source of all creation;
all-pervasive, omnipotent, eternal;
may the Goddess,
the lady of the moon;
and the God,
horned hunter of the sun;
may the powers of the spirits of the stones,

rulers of the elemental realms;
may the powers of the stars above and the earth below,
bless this place, and this time, and I who am with you. *

The Simple Feast

Hold up a cup of wine or some other liquid between your hands to the sky, and say:

Gracious Goddess of abundance,
bless this wine and infuse it with your love.
In your names, Mother Goddess and Father God,
I bless this wine (or brew, juice, etc.).

Hold up a plate of cakes (bread, biscuits) with both hands to the sky and say:

Powerful God of the harvest,
bless these cakes and infuse them with your love.
In your names, Mother Goddess and Father God,
I bless these cakes (or this bread). †

Consecration of Tools

Light the candles. Set the incense smoking. Cast the circle of stones. Place the tool on the pentacle, or a plate of salt. Touch it with the point of the magic knife (or your projective hand) and say:

I consecrate you, O knife of steel (or wand of wood, etc.)
to cleanse and purify you to serve me within the circle of stones.
In the names of the Mother Goddess and Father God,
you are consecrated.

---

* The Blessing Chant can be said at the beginning of any type of ritual as a general invocation. Separate invocations of the Goddess and God may follow.

† The Simple Feast is usually held at the end of the sabbats and esbats. It is a sedate version of the wild feasts once held during agricultural rituals in rural Europe. Many liquids other than wine can be used; see the recipes section.

Send projective energy into the tool, cleansing it of all negativity and past associations. Now pick it up and sprinkle with salt, pass it through the incense smoke, through the candle flame, and sprinkle with water, calling upon the spirits of the stones to consecrate it.

Then hold the tool to the sky, saying:

> *I charge you by the Old Ones:*
> *by the omnipotent Goddess and God:*
> *by the virtues of the sun, moon, and stars:*
> *by the powers of the earth, air, fire, and water,*
> *that I shall obtain all that I desire through you.*
> *Charge this by your power, Old Ones!**

The tool should immediately be put to use to strengthen and bind the consecration. For example, the athame can be used to consecrate another tool; a wand to invoke the Goddess; the pentacle to act as a resting place for a tool during its consecration.

The Full Moon Rite

Perform this at night, in view of the moon, if possible. It is appropriate for crescents, white flowers, silver, and other lunar symbols to be present on the altar for this ritual. The quartz crystal sphere can be placed on the altar as well. Or, if you prefer, use the cauldron (or a small white or silver bowl) filled with water. Place a piece of silver into the water.

Arrange the altar, light the candles and censer, and cast the circle of stones.

Stand before the altar and invoke the Goddess and God, with the Blessing Chant and/or any other invocations (see "Prayers, Chants, and Invocations" in this Book of Shadows).

Now gaze at the moon, if possible. Feel its energies sinking into your body. Feel its cool Goddess energy wash you with power and love.

---

* The words used in this consecration rite are based on one included in *The Key of Solomon*, and are similar to those used in many Wiccan traditions.

Now say these or similar words:

Wondrous lady of the moon
You who greets the dusk with silvered kisses;
mistress of the night and of all magics,
who rides the clouds in blackened skies
and spills light upon the cold earth;
O lunar Goddess,
crescented-one,
shadow maker and shadow breaker;
revealer of mysteries past and present;
puller of seas and ruler of women;
all-wise lunar Mother,
I greet your celestial jewel
at the waxing of its powers
with a rite in your honor.
I pray by the moon,
I pray by the moon,
I pray by the moon.

Continue chanting "I pray by the moon" for as long as you will. Visualize the Goddess if you so desire, perhaps as a tall, robust woman wearing silver jewelry and white, rippling, draped clothing. A crescent moon may rest upon her brow, or she may toss a glowing, silvery white orb in her hands. She trods the starfield of eternal night in an eternal round with her lover, the sun God, spreading moon rays wherever she goes. Her eyes laugh, her skin is white and translucent. She glows.

Now is the time for magic of all types, for the full of the moon marks the height of its powers, and all positive spells cast then are powerful.

Full moons are also excellent times for meditation, mirror magic, and psychic workings, for such are often more successful within the circle. Crystal scrying is particularly recommended; flood the crystal with moonlight prior to the ritual. If you have no crystal sphere, use the cauldron filled with water and the piece of silver. Gaze at the water (or at the moon glinting on the silver) to awaken your psychic awareness.

Lunar liquids such as lemonade, milk, or white wine can be consumed during The Simple Feast that follows. Crescent cakes are traditional as well. Thank the Goddess and God and release the circle. It is done.

The Seasonal Festivals

Yule
(Circa December 21)

The altar is adorned with evergreens such as pine, rosemary, bay, juniper, and cedar, and the same can be laid to mark the circle of stones. Dried leaves can also be placed on the altar.

The cauldron, resting on the altar on a heat-proof surface (or placed before it if too large), should be filled with ignitable spirit (alcohol), or a red candle can be placed within it. At outdoor rites, lay a fire within the cauldron to be lit during ritual.

Arrange the altar, light the candles and incense, and cast the circle of stones. Recite the Blessing Chant, page 132. Invoke the Goddess and God.* Stand before the cauldron and gaze within it. Say these or similar words:

> *I sorrow not, though the world is wrapped in sleep.*
> *I sorrow not, though the icy winds blast.*
> *I sorrow not, though the snow falls hard and deep.*
> *I sorrow not; this too shall soon be past.*

Ignite the cauldron (or candle), using long matches or a taper. As the flame(s) leap up say:

> *I light this fire in your honor, Mother Goddess.*
> *You have created life from death; warmth from cold;*
> *the sun lives once again; the time of light is waxing.*

---

* Using, once again, any of the invocations found in "Prayers, Chants, and Invocations," page 153, or your own words.

Welcome, ever-returning God of the sun!
Hail Mother of all!

Circle the altar and cauldron slowly, clockwise, watching the flames. Say the following chant for some time:

The wheel turns; the power burns.

Meditate upon the sun, on the hidden energies lying dormant in winter, not only in the earth but within ourselves. Think of birth not as the start of life but as its continuance. Welcome the return of the God.

After a time cease and stand once again before the altar and flaming cauldron. Say:

Great God of the sun,
I welcome your return.
May you shine brightly upon the Goddess;
may you shine brightly upon the earth,
scattering seeds and fertilizing the land.
All blessings upon you,
reborn one of the sun!

Works of magic, if necessary, may follow. Celebrate The Simple Feast. The circle is released.

Yule Lore
One traditional Yuletide practice is the creation of a Yule tree. This can be a living, potted tree that can later be planted in the ground, or a cut one. The choice is yours.

Appropriate Wiccan decorations are fun to make, from strings of dried rosebuds and cinnamon sticks (or popcorn and cranberries) for garlands, to bags of fragrant spices that are hung from boughs. Quartz crystals can be wrapped with shiny wire and suspended from sturdy branches to resemble icicles. Apples, oranges, and lemons hanging from boughs are strikingly beautiful, natural decorations, and were customary in ancient times.

Many enjoy the custom of lighting the Yule log. This is a graphic representation of the rebirth of the God within the sacred fire of the

Mother Goddess. If you choose to burn one, select a proper log (traditionally of oak or pine). Carve or chalk a figure of the sun (such as a rayed disc) or the God (a horned circle or a figure of a man) upon it, with the white-handled knife, and set it alight in the fireplace at dusk on Yule. As the log burns, visualize the sun shining within it and think of the coming warmer days.

As to food, nuts, fruits such as apples and pears, cakes of carraways soaked in cider, and (for nonvegetarians) pork are traditional fare. Wassail, lambswool, hibiscus, or ginger tea are fine drinks for The Simple Feast or Yule meals.

Imbolc

(February 2)

A symbol of the season, such as a representation of a snowflake, a white flower, or perhaps some snow in a crystal container can be placed on the altar. An orange candle anointed with musk, cinnamon, frankincense, or rosemary oil, unlit, should also be there. Snow can be melted and used for the water during the circle casting.

Arrange the altar, light the candles and censer, and cast the circle of stones. Recite the Blessing Chant, page 132. Invoke the Goddess and God. Say such words as the following:

> *This is the time of the feast of torches,*
> *when every lamp blazes and shines*
> *to welcome the rebirth of the God.*
> *I celebrate the Goddess, I celebrate the God;*
> *all the earth celebrates*
> *beneath its mantle of sleep.*

Light the orange taper from the red candle on the altar (or at the southern point of the circle). Slowly walk the circle clockwise, bearing the candle before you. Say these or similar words:

> *All the land is wrapped in winter.*
> *The air is chilled and*
> *frost envelopes the earth.*

But Lord of the sun,
horned one of animals and wild places,
unseen you have been reborn
of the gracious Mother Goddess,
lady of all fertility.
Hail great God!
Hail and welcome!

Stop before the altar, holding aloft the candle. Gaze at its flame. Visualize your life blossoming with creativity, with renewed energy and strength.

If you need to look into the future or past, now is an ideal time. Works of magic, if necessary, may follow. Celebrate The Simple Feast. The circle is released.

Imbolc Lore

It is traditional upon Imbolc, at sunset or just after ritual, to light every lamp in the house—if only for a few moments. Or, light candles in each room in honor of the sun's rebirth. Alternately, light a kerosene lamp with a red chimney and place this in a prominent part of the home or in a window.

If snow lies on the ground outside, walk in it for a moment, recalling the warmth of summer. With your projective hand, trace an image of the sun on the snow.

Foods appropriate to eat on this day include those from the dairy, since Imbolc marks the festival of calving. Sour cream dishes are fine. Spicy and full-bodied foods in honor of the sun are equally attuned. Curries and all dishes made with peppers, onions, leeks, shallots, garlic or chives are appropriate. Spiced wines and dishes containing raisins— all foods symbolic of the sun—are also traditional.

Ostara

(Circa March 21)

Flowers should be laid on the altar, placed around the circle and strewn on the ground. The cauldron can be filled with spring water and flowers, and buds and blossoms may be worn as well. A small potted plant should be placed on the altar.

Arrange the altar, light the candles and incense, and cast the circle of stones. Recite the Blessing Chant, page 132. Invoke the Goddess and God in whatever words please you. Stand before the altar and gaze upon the plant as you say:

O great Goddess,
you have freed yourself from the icy prison of winter.
Now is the greening, when the fragrance of flowers drifts on the breeze.
This is the beginning.
Life renews itself by your magic, earth Goddess.
The God stretches and rises, eager in his youth,
and bursting with the promise of summer.

Touch the plant. Connect with its energies and, through it, all nature. Travel inside its leaves and stems through your visualization—from the center of your consciousness out through your arm and fingers and into the plant itself. Explore its inner nature; sense the miraculous processes of life at work within it. After a time, still touching the plant, say:

I walk the earth in friendship, not in dominance.
Mother Goddess and Father God,
instill within me through this plant a
warmth for all living things.
Teach me to revere the earth and all its treasures.
May I never forget.

Meditate upon the changing of the seasons. Feel the rousing of energies around you in the earth. Works of magic, if necessary, may follow. Celebrate The Simple Feast. The circle is released.

Ostara Lore

A traditional vernal equinox pastime: go to a field and randomly collect wildflowers.* Or, buy some from a florist, taking one or two of those that appeal to you. Then bring them home and divine their magical meanings by the use of books, your own intuition, a pendulum, or by other means. The flowers you've chosen reveal your inner thoughts and emotions.

It is important at this time of renewed life to plan a walk (or a ride) through gardens, a park, woodlands, forest, and other green places. This is not simply exercise, and you should be on no other mission. It isn't even just an appreciation of nature. Make your walk celebratory, a ritual for nature itself.

Other traditional activities include planting seeds, working on magical gardens, and practicing all forms of herb work—magical, medicinal, cosmetic, culinary, and artistic.

Foods in tune with this day (linking your meals with the seasons is a fine method of attuning with nature) include those made of seeds, such as sunflower, pumpkin, and sesame seeds, as well as pine nuts. Sprouts are equally appropriate, as are leafy, green vegetables. Flower dishes such as stuffed nasturtiums or carnation cupcakes also find their place here.†

---

* Thank the flowers for their sacrifice before picking them, using a collection formula such as can be found in "An Herbal Grimoire" elsewhere in this Book of Shadows.

† Find a book of flower cooking or simply make spice cupcakes. Ice with pink frosting and place a fresh carnation petal on each cupcake. Stuff nasturtium blossoms with a mixture made of cream cheese, chopped nuts, chives, and watercress. They're hot!

Beltane

(April 30 or May 1)

If possible, celebrate Beltane in a forest or near a living tree. If this is impossible, bring a small tree within the circle, preferably potted; it can be of any type.

Create a small token or charm in honor of the wedding of the Goddess and God to hang upon the tree. You can make several if you desire. These tokens can be bags filled with fragrant flowers, strings of beads, carvings, flower garlands—whatever your talents and imagination can conjure.

Arrange the altar, light the candles and censer, and cast the circle of stones. Recite the Blessing Chant, page 132. Invoke the Goddess and God. Stand before the altar and say, with wand upraised:

> *O Mother Goddess,*
> *queen of the night and of the earth;*
> *O Father God, king of the day and of the forests,*
> *I celebrate your union as nature rejoices*
> *in a riotous blaze of color and life.*
> *Accept my gift, Mother Goddess*
> *and Father God, in honor of your union.*

Place the token(s) on the tree.

> *From your mating shall spring forth life anew;*
> *a profusion of living creatures shall cover the lands,*
> *and the winds will blow pure and sweet.*
> *O ancient ones, I celebrate with you!*

Works of magic, if necessary, may follow. Celebrate The Simple Feast. The circle is released.

Beltane Lore

Weaving and plaiting are traditional arts at this time of year, for the joining together of two substances to form a third is in the spirit of Beltane.

Foods traditionally come from the dairy, and dishes such as marigold custard (see Recipes, starting on page 161) and vanilla ice cream are fine. Oatmeal cakes are also appropriate.

Midsummer
(Circa June 21)

Before the rite, make up a small cloth pouch filled with herbs such as lavender, chamomile, St. John's wort, vervain, or any of the Midsummer herbs listed in "An Herbal Grimoire," page 167. Mentally pour all your troubles, problems, pains, sorrows, and illnesses, if any, into this petition as you construct it. Tie it shut with a red string. Place this on the altar for use during the rite. The cauldron should also be there or nearby. Even if you use candles to mark the quarters, the red candle in a holder should also be on the altar. For outdoor rituals, light a fire— however small— and drop the pouch into this.

Arrange the altar, light the candles and censer, and cast the circle of stones. Recite the Blessing Chant, page 132. Invoke the Goddess and God. Stand before the altar and say, with wand upraised:

> *I celebrate the noon of summer with mystic rites.*
> *O great Goddess and God,*
> *all nature vibrates with your energies*
> *and the earth is bathed with warmth and life.*
> *Now is the time of forgetting past cares and banes;*
> *now is the time for purification.*
> *O fiery sun, burn away the unuseful, the hurtful,*
> *the bane, in your omnipotent power.*
> *Purify me! Purify me! Purify me!*

Lay the wand on the altar. Take up the herbal petition and light it in the red candle on the altar (or, if outdoors, the ritual fire). When it is burning, drop it into the cauldron (or some other heat-proof container) and say:

> *I banish you by the powers of the Goddess and God!*
> *I banish you by the powers of the sun, moon and stars!*
> *I banish you by the powers of earth, air, fire, and water!*

Pause, seeing the hurts and pains burning into nothingness. Then say:

> *O gracious Goddess, O gracious God,*
> *on this night of Midsummer magic*
> *I pray that you charge my life with wonder and joy.*
> *Help me in attuning with*
> *the energies adrift on the enchanted night air.*
> *I give thanks.*

Reflect upon the purification you have undergone. Feel the powers of nature flowing through you, washing you clean with divine energy.

Works of magic, if necessary, may follow. Celebrate The Simple Feast. The circle is released.

Midsummer Lore

Midsummer is practically the classic time to perform magics of all kinds. Healings, love magic, and protections are especially suitable. Herbs can be dried over the ritual fire if you're celebrating outdoors. Leap the fire for purification and renewed energy.

Fresh fruits are standard fare for Midsummer.

Lughnasadh
(August 1)

Place upon the altar sheaves of wheat, barley or oats, fruit and breads, perhaps a loaf fashioned in the figure of the sun or a man to represent the God. Corn dollies, symbolic of the Goddess, can be present there as well.

Arrange the altar, light the candles and censer, and cast the circle of stones. Recite the Blessing Chant, page 132. Invoke the Goddess and God. Stand before the altar, holding aloft the sheaves of grain, saying these or similar words:

> *Now is the time of the first harvest,*
> *when the bounties of nature give of themselves*
> *so that we may survive.*

O God of the ripening fields, lord of the grain,
grant me the understanding of sacrifice as you prepare
to deliver yourself under the sickle of the Goddess
and journey to the lands of eternal summer.
O Goddess of the dark moon, teach me the secrets of rebirth
as the sun loses its strength and the nights grow cold.

Rub the heads of the wheat with your fingers so that the grains fall onto the altar. Lift a piece of fruit and bite it, savoring its flavor, and say:

I partake of the first harvest,
mixing its energies with mine
that I may continue my quest for the starry
wisdom of perfection.
O lady of the moon and lord of the sun,
gracious ones before whom the stars halt their courses,
I offer my thanks for the continuing fertility of the earth.
May the nodding grain loose its seeds to be buried
in the Mother's breast,
ensuring rebirth in the warmth
of the coming spring.

Consume the rest of the fruit. Works of magic, if necessary, may follow. Celebrate The Simple Feast. The circle is released.

Lughnasadh Lore

It is appropriate to plant the seeds from the fruit consumed in ritual. If they sprout, grow the plant with love and as a symbol of your connection with the Goddess and God.

Wheat weaving (the making of corn dollies, etc.) is an appropriate activity for Lughnasadh. Visits to fields, orchards, lakes, and wells are also traditional.

The foods of Lughnasadh include bread, blackberries and all berries, acorns (leached of their poisons first), crab apples, all grains, and locally ripe produce. A cake is sometimes baked, and cider is used in place of wine.

If you do make a figure of the God from bread, it can be used for The Simple Feast.

Mabon

(Circa September 21)

Decorate the altar with acorns, oak sprigs, pine and cypress cones, ears of corn, wheat stalks, and other fruits and nuts. Also place there a small rustic basket filled with dried leaves of various colors and kinds.

Arrange the altar, light the candles and censer, and cast the circle of stones. Recite the Blessing Chant, page 132. Invoke the Goddess and God. Stand before the altar, holding aloft the basket of leaves, and slowly scatter them so that they cascade to the ground within the circle. Say such words as these:

Leaves fall,
the days grow cold.
The Goddess pulls her mantle of earth around her as
you, O great sun God, sail toward the west
to the lands of eternal enchantment,
wrapped in the coolness of night.
Fruits ripen, seeds drop,
the hours of day and night are balanced.
Chill winds blow in from the north wailing laments.
In this seeming extinction of nature's power,
O blessed Goddess, I know that life continues.
For spring is impossible without the second harvest,
as surely as life is impossible without death.
Blessings upon you, O fallen God,
as you journey into the lands of winter
and into the Goddess' loving arms.

Place the basket down and say:

O gracious Goddess of all fertility,
I have sown and reaped the fruits of my actions, good and bane.
Grant me the courage to plant seeds of joy and love in
the coming year, banishing misery and hate.
Teach me the secrets
of wise existence upon this planet,
O luminous one of the night!

Works of magic, if necessary, may follow. Celebrate The Simple Feast. The circle is released.

Mabon Lore

A traditional practice is to walk wild places and forests, gathering seed pods and dried plants. Some of these can be used to decorate the home; others saved for future herbal magic.

The foods of Mabon consist of the second harvest's gleanings, so grains, fruits, and vegetables predominate, especially corn. Corn bread is traditional fare, as are beans and baked squash.

Samhain
(October 31)

Place upon the altar apples, pomegranates, pumpkins, squashes, and other late autumn fruits. Autumn flowers such as marigolds and chrysanthemums are fine too. Write on a piece of paper an aspect of your life that you wish to be free of: anger, a baneful habit, misplaced feelings, disease. The cauldron or some similar tool must be present before the altar as well, on a trivet or some other heat-proof surface (if the legs aren't long enough). A small, flat dish marked with an eight-spoked wheel symbol should also be there.*

Prior to the ritual, sit quietly and think of friends and loved ones who have passed away. Do not despair. Know that they have gone on to greater things. Keep firmly in mind that the physical isn't the absolute reality, and that souls never die.

Arrange the altar, light the candles and censer, and cast the circle of stones. Recite the Blessing Chant, page 132. Invoke the Goddess and God.

Lift one of the pomegranates and, with your freshly-washed white-handled knife, pierce the skin of the fruit. Remove several seeds and place them on the wheel-marked dish. Raise your wand, face the altar, and say:

---

* This is just what it sounds like. On a flat plate or dish, paint a large circle. Put a dot in the center of this circle and paint eight spokes radiating out from the dot to the larger circle. Thus, you have a wheel symbol—a symbol of the sabbats, a symbol of timelessness.

On this night of Samhain
I mark your passing, O sun king,
through the sunset into the land of the young.
I mark also the passing of all who have gone before,
and all who will go after.
O gracious Goddess, eternal Mother,
you who gives birth to the fallen,
teach me to know that in the time of the greatest darkness
there is the greatest light.

Taste the pomegranate seeds; burst them with your teeth and savor their sharp, bittersweet flavor. Look down at the eight-spoked symbol on the plate; the wheel of the year, the cycle of the seasons, the end and beginning of all creation. Light a fire within the cauldron (a candle is fine). Sit before it, holding the piece of paper, gazing at its flames. Say:

Wise one of the waning moon,
Goddess of the starry night,
I create this fire within your cauldron
to transform that which is plaguing me.
May the energies be reversed: from darkness, light!
From bane, good! From death, birth!

Light the paper in the cauldron's flames and drop it inside. As it burns, know that your ill diminishes, lessens, and finally leaves you as it is consumed within the universal fires.*

If you wish, you may attempt scrying or some other form of divination, for this is a perfect time to look into the past or future. Try to recall past lives too, if you will. But leave the dead in peace. Honor them with your memories but do not call them to you.†

---

* The cauldron, seen as the Goddess.

† Many Wiccans do attempt to communicate with their deceased ancestors and friends at this time, but it seems to me that if we accept the doctrine of reincarnation, this is a rather strange practice. Perhaps the *personalities* that we knew still exist, but if the *soul* is currently incarnate in another body, communication would be difficult, to say the least. Thus, it seems best to remember them with peace and love—but not to call them up.

Release any pain and sense of loss you may feel into the cauldron's flames.

Works of magic, if necessary, may follow. Celebrate The Simple Feast. The circle is released.

Samhain Lore

It is traditional on Samhain night to leave a plate of food outside the home for the souls of the dead. A candle placed in the window guides them to the lands of eternal summer, and burying apples in the hard-packed earth "feeds" the passed ones on their journey.

For food, beets, turnips, apples, corn, nuts, gingerbread, cider, mulled wines, and pumpkin dishes are appropriate, as are meat dishes (once again, if you're not vegetarian; if you are, tofu seems ritually correct).

A Ritual of Gestures*

STAND IN THE ritual area. Still your thoughts. Breathe deeply for half a minute or so until composed and calm. Turn your mind to our deities.

Face north. Lift both hands to waist height, palms down. Press your fingers together, creating two solid, flat planes. Sense solidity, foundation, fertility. Invoke the powers of *earth* through the gesture.

Moments later, turn toward the east. Raise your hands a foot higher, your palms facing away from you (no longer parallel with the ground), and elbows slightly bent. Spread your fingers and hold this position, sensing movement and communication. Invoke the forces of *air* through the gesture.

Face south. Lift your hands fully above your head. Keeping the elbows straight, grasp your fingers into tight fists. Feel force, power, creation, and destruction. Invoke the forces of *fire* through the gesture.

Turn to the west. Lower your hands a foot or so. Bend the elbows, turn your palms upward and cup them, pressing the thumbs against the forefingers. Sense fluidity, the ocean, liquidity. Invoke the forces of *water* through the gesture.

Face north again. Throw your head back and raise both hands to the sky, palms up, fingers spread. Drink in the essence of The One, the

---

* As mentioned in chapter 5, gestures can be potent tools for slipping into ritual consciousness. After rereading that chapter I had the idea to compose an entire ritual of gestures, using no physical tools, no words, no music, or even visualizations. This is merely a suggestion as to its form, and has plenty of possibilities for expansion. It is to be used for attunement with The One, the Goddess and God, and the elemental forces, not for magic or seasonal observances.

unknowable, unapproachable ultimate source of all. Sense the mysteries within the universe.

Lower your projective hand but keep your receptive hand high. Pressing the third, fourth, and fifth fingers against the palm, lift the forefinger and thumb to create a rough crescent shape. Sense the reality of the Goddess. Sense her love, her fertility, her compassion. Sense the powers of the moon in the gesture; the force of the eternal seas—the presence of the Goddess.

Lower your receptive hand; lift your projective hand. Bend down the middle and fourth fingers toward the palm, and trap them with the thumb. Lift the forefinger and little finger up to the sky, creating a horned image. Sense the reality of the God. Sense the power of the sun in the gesture; the untamed energies of the woodlands—the presence of the God.

Lower your projective hand. Lie down flat. Spread your legs and arms until you've created the pattern of a pentagram. Sense the powers of the elements running through you; merging and coalescing into your being. Sense them as emanations from The One, the Goddess, and God.

Meditate. Commune. Communicate.

When finished, simply stand up. Your rite of gestures is over.

The Law of the Power

The Power shall not be used to bring harm, to injure or control others. But if the need rises, the Power shall be used to protect your life or the lives of others.

The Power is used only as need dictates.

The Power can be used for your own gain, as long as by doing so you harm none.

It is unwise to accept money for use of the Power, for it quickly controls its taker. Be not as those of other religions.

Use not the Power for prideful gain, for such cheapens the mysteries of Wicca and magic.

Ever remember that the Power is the sacred gift of the Goddess and God, and should never be misused or abused.

And this is the Law of the Power.

Invocation of the Elements

Air, fire, water, earth, elements of astral birth,
I call you now; attend to me!
In the circle, rightly cast,
safe from psychic curse or blast,
I call you now; attend to me!
From cave and desert, sea and hill,
by wand, blade, cup, and pentacle,
I call you now; attend to me!
*This is my will, so mote it be!**

Prayers, Chants, and Invocations of and to the Goddess and God

These prayers can be used to invoke the Goddess and God during ritual, just after the cirde casting. Of course, any that you compose or are inspired to say can be used as well.

A few chants are also included to raise energy or to commune with the deities.

Some of these invocations rhyme, and some do not. This simply speaks of my ability to compose rhyme, I suppose. But recall the power of rhyme—it links our conscious mind to the unconscious or psychic mind, thereby producing ritual consciousness.

Some of these are related to specific deities but, as Dion Fortune wrote, "All the gods are one god; and all the goddesses are one goddess, and there is one initiator."†

---

* This invocation may be chanted while moving or dancing around the altar to raise elemental energy for magical workings.

† *Aspects of Occultism.* London: Aquarian Press, 1962, page 35.

Invocation to the Goddess

Crescent one of the starry skies,
flowered one of the fertile plain,
flowing one of the ocean's sighs,
blessed one of the gentle rain;
hear my chant 'midst the standing stones,
open me to your mystic light;
waken me to your silver tones,
be with me in my sacred rite!

Invocation to Pan

O great God Pan,
beast and man,
shepherd of goats and lord of the land,
I call you to attend my rites
on this most magical of nights.
God of the wine,
God of the vine,
God of the fields and God of the kine,
attend my circle with your love
and send your blessings from above.
Help me to heal;
help me to feel;
help me to bring forth love and weal.
Pan of the forests, Pan of the glade,
be with me as my magic is made!

Isis Invocation

Isis of the moon, you who are all that ever was,
all that is, and all that shall be:
come, veiled queen of night!
Come as the scent of the sacred lotus charging my circle
with love and magic.
Do descend upon my circle, I pray,
O blessed Isis!

Prayer to the Horned God

Horned one of the wilderness,
winged one of the shining skies,
rayed one of the splen'drous sun,
fallen one of the Samhain cries—
I call amidst the standing stones
praying that you, O ancient one,
will deign to bless my mystic rites—
O fiery lord of the blazing sun!

New Moon Chant to Diana

Waxing, waxing, growing, growing—
Diana's power is flowing, flowing.
(repeat)

Call to the God

Ancient God of the forest deeps,
master of beast and sun;
here where the world is hushed and sleeps
now that the day is done.
I call you in the ancient way
here in my circle round,
asking that you will hear me pray
and send your sun force down.

Invocation to the Goddess

Gracious Goddess,
you who are the queen of the gods,
the lamp of night,
the creator of all that is wild and free;
mother of woman and man;
lover of the horned God and protectress of all the Wicca:
descend, I pray, with your lunar ray of power upon my circle here!

Invocation to the God

Blazing God,
you who are the king of the gods, lord of the sun,
master of all that is wild and free;
father of woman and man,
lover of the moon goddess and protector of all the Wicca:
descend, I pray, with your solar ray of power upon my circle here!

Goddess Chant

Luna, luna, luna, Diana
luna, luna, luna, Diana
bless me, bless me, bless me, Diana,
luna, luna, luna, Diana (repeat)

Evening Chant to the God

Hail fair sun,
ruler of day;
rise on the morn
to light my way.
(to be said while watching the sunset)

Evening Chant to the Goddess

Hail fair moon,
ruler of night
guard me and mine
until the light.
(to be said while moon-gazing at night)

Goddess Chant

Aaaaaaaaaaaaaah

Ooooooooooooooh

Uuuuuuuuuuuuu

Eeeeeeeeeeeeeeee

*Iiiiiiiiiiiiiiiiiiiiii**

---

* These are, obviously, the vowels of the English language. Pronounce them as A–"Ah," O–"Oh," U–"Oo," E–"E," I–"Eye." Extend the vowels. As you vocalize them, stretch the sounds. This produces Goddess awareness, and rouses the psychic mind.

The Lore of Numbers

To be used in ritual and magical workings. In general, odd numbers are related to women, receptive energy, and the Goddess; even numbers to men, projective energy, and the God.

1—The universe; The One; the source of all.

2—The Goddess and God; The perfect duality; projective and receptive energy; the couple; personal union with deity; interpenetration of the physical and spiritual; balance.

3—The triple Goddess; the lunar phases; the physical, mental, and spiritual aspects of our species.

4—The elements; the spirits of the stones; the winds; the seasons.

5—The senses; the pentagram; the elements plus akasha; a Goddess number.

7—The planets that the ancients knew; the time of the lunar phase; power; protection and magic.

8—The number of the sabbats; a number of the God.

9—A number of the Goddess.

13—The number of esbats; a fortunate number.

15—A number of good fortune.

21—The number of sabbats and moons in the Wiccan year; a number of the Goddess.

28—A number of the moon; a number of the Goddess.

101—The number of fertility.

The planets are numbered thus:

Saturn, 3	Venus, 7
Jupiter, 4	Mercury, 8
Mars, 5	Moon, 9*
Sun, 6	

---

* There are many variants of this system. This is simply the one that I use.

Thirteen Goals of a Witch

    I. Know yourself
   II. Know your Craft (Wicca)
  III. Learn
  IV. Apply knowledge with wisdom
   V. Achieve balance
  VI. Keep your words in good order
 VII. Keep your thoughts in good order
VIII. Celebrate life
  IX. Attune with the cycles of the earth
   X. Breathe and eat correctly
  XI. Exercise the body
 XII. Meditate
XIII. Honor the Goddess and God

Recipes

Recipes for Food

Crescent Cakes
1 cup finely ground almonds
1¼ cups flour
½ cup confectioner's sugar
2 drops almond extract
½ cup butter, softened
1 egg yolk

Combine almonds, flour, sugar, and extract until thoroughly mixed. With the hands, work in butter and egg yolk until well blended. Chill dough. Preheat oven to 325 degrees F. Pinch off pieces of dough about the size of walnuts and shape into crescents. Place on greased sheets and bake for about 20 minutes. Serve during The Simple Feast, especially at esbats.*

Beltane Marigold Custard
2 cups milk
1 cup unsprayed marigold petals
¼ tsp. salt
3 tbsp. sugar
1- to 2-inch piece vanilla bean

---

* This is the best recipe I've been able to find. Most of the other published ones taste foul. Purists who worry about the inclusion of sugar in this recipe needn't. It's ritually related to Venus and has a long magical history.

3 egg yolks, slightly beaten

⅛ tsp. allspice

⅛ tsp. nutmeg

½ tsp. rose water

whipped cream

Using a clean mortar and pestle reserved for cooking purposes, pound marigold petals. Or, crush with a spoon. Mix the salt, sugar, and spices together. Scald milk with the marigolds and the vanilla bean. Remove the vanilla bean and add the slightly beaten yolks and dry ingredients. Cook on low heat. When the mixture coats a spoon, add rose water and cool.

Top with whipped cream, garnish with fresh marigold petals.

Soft Mead

1 quart water, preferably spring water

1 cup honey

1 sliced lemon

½ tsp. nutmeg

Boil together all ingredients in a nonmetallic pot. While boiling, scrape off the rising "scum" with a wooden spoon. When no more rises add the following:

pinch salt

juice of ½ lemon

Strain and cool. Drink in place of alcoholic mead or wine during The Simple Feast.

Recipes for Incenses

To make incenses, simply grind the ingredients and mix them together. As you mix, sense their energies. Burn on charcoal blocks in the censer during ritual. See appendix 1, page 201, for suppliers of herbs and charcoal.

Circle Incense

4 parts frankincense

2 parts myrrh

2 parts benzoin

1 part sandalwood

½ part cinnamon

½ part rose petals

¼ part vervain

¼ part rosemary

¼ part bay

Burn in the circle for all types of rituals and spells. Frankincense, myrrh, and benzoin should definitely constitute the bulk of the mixture.

Altar Incense

3 parts frankincense

2 parts myrrh

1 part cinnamon

Burn as a general incense on the altar to purify it and to promote ritual consciousness during rituals.

Full Moon Ritual Incense

2 parts sandalwood

2 parts frankincense

½ part gardenia petals

¼ part rose petals

a few drops ambergris oil

Burn during esbats or simply at the time of the full moon to attune with the Goddess.

Spring Sabbat Incense
   3 parts frankincense
   2 parts sandalwood
   1 part benzoin
   1 part cinnamon
   a few drops patchouli oil

   Burn during spring and summer sabbat rituals.

Fall Sabbat Incense
   3 parts frankincense
   2 parts myrrh
   1 part rosemary
   1 part cedar
   1 part juniper

   Burn during fall and winter sabbat rituals.

Recipes for Oils

To create oils, simply mix them in a bottle. Wear for ritual purposes. See appendix 1, page 201, for suppliers.

Sabbat Oil No. 1
   3 parts patchouli
   2 parts musk
   1 part carnation

   Wear to the sabbats to promote communion with the deities.

Sabbat Oil No. 2
   2 parts frankincense
   1 part myrrh
   1 part allspice
   1 drop clove

   Use as the above formula.

Full Moon Oil No. 1

3 parts rose
1 part jasmine
1 part sandalwood

Anoint the body prior to esbats to attune with lunar energies.

Full Moon Oil No. 2

3 parts sandalwood
2 parts lemon
1 part rose

Another like the above.

Goddess Oil

3 parts rose
2 parts tuberose
1 part lemon
1 part palmarosa
1 part ambergris

Wear to honor the Goddess during rituals.

Horned God Oil

2 parts frankincense
2 parts cinnamon
1 part bay
1 part rosemary
1 part musk

Wear to honor the horned God during rituals.

Altar Oil

4 parts frankincense
3 parts myrrh
1 part galangal
1 part vervain
1 part lavender

Anoint the altar with this oil at regular intervals to purify and empower it.

An Herbal Grimoire

A guide to the use of herbs and plants in Wiccan ritual

Of Gathering Flowers, Herbs, and Plants

Before cutting with the white-handled knife, attune with the plant through visualization. Feel its energies. As you cut, say these or similar words:

O little plant of (name, such as hyssop, etc.)
I ask that you give of your bounty that it may aid me in my work.
Grow stronger by my stroke, stronger and more powerful,
O plant of (name)*!*

If it is a tree, substitute the appropriate word (tree of oak). Gently cut only what you need, and never from very young plants or more than 25 percent of the growth. At the base of the plant, leave an offering: a silver coin, a bright jewel, a bit of wine or milk, grain, a quartz crystal, and so on. Cover the offering and it is done.

Of the Circle

The magic circle may be fashioned with garlands of flowers sacred to the Goddess and God. Alternately, flowers can be scattered around the perimeter of the circle.

The point stones may be ringed with fresh flowers and herbs suitable to the elements, such as:

North: corn, cypress, fern, honeysuckle, wheat, vervain

East: acacia, bergamot, clover, dandelion, lavender, lemon grass, mint, mistletoe, parsley, pine

South: basil, carnation, cedar, chrysanthemum, dill, ginger, heliotrope, holly, juniper, marigold, peppermint

West: apple blossoms, lemon balm, camellia, catnip, daffodil, elder, gardenia, grape, heather, hibiscus, jasmine, orchid

Fresh flowers may be present on the altar or, if none are available, greens such as ferns may be used.

When casting the circle around a tree, you can use the fruit, leaves, nuts, or flowers of that tree to mark out the circle, if desired.

All of these can be used in addition to the cord and stones.

Of the Balefire

If you wish to build a fire for an outdoor ritual, it can be composed of all or any combination of the following woods:

Apple	Oak
Cedar	Pine
Dogwood	Poplar
Juniper	Rowan
Mesquite	

If these are unavailable, use native woods. Rites performed on the seashore can be illuminated with balefires of dried driftwood collected prior to the rite.

Of the Home Circle

Magical plants growing outside the home in containers can be placed around the circle or on the altar during ritual. If you primarily work indoors, choose an odd-numbered selection of sacred plants and grow these in your ritual area. If they need more sunlight, simply move them outdoors and bring inside during ritual. Give them energy and love, and they'll aid you in your worship and magic.

Though any but poisonous plants can be used, such plants as these are recommended:

African violets

Red geraniums

Cacti (all types)

Ferns (all types)

Holly

Hyssop

Palms (all types)

Rose

Rose geranium

Rosemary

Ti (*Cord yline terminalis*)

Wax plant (*Hoya carnosa*)

Of the Celebrant

Wear fresh flowers and herbs in your hair and on your body, if you prefer, during the rites. Crowns or chaplets of flowers are always appropriate for spring and summer rites. Wear oak and pine during the winter rituals.

You may wish to wear a necklace of herbs and seeds, such as tonka beans, whole nutmegs, star anise, acorns, and other seeds and nuts, strung on a natural fiber. Strings of small pine cones may also be worn.

For full moon rituals held at night, wear night-blooming, fragrant flowers to suffuse yourself with lunar energies.

Of the Tools

These are suggestions for dedicating the tools prior to their first use or formal consecration, if any. Perform these with proper visualization and ritual intent.

The Magic Knife or Sword

Rub the blade with fresh basil, rosemary, or oak leaves, at sunrise, outdoors where you will not be disturbed or seen. Lay the sword or knife on the ground with its point to the south. Walk clockwise around it thrice, scattering bay leaves (preferably fresh) over it. Take up the sword or knife, stand facing east and, holding it upward but with arms lowered, invoke the God to infuse your knife or sword with his strength. Point it to the sky, invoking the Goddess to charge your blade with her love and power.

Wrap your knife or sword in red cloth and take it home. It may be stored in the cloth, if desired.

The White-Handled Knife

Early in the morning, go to a forest (or park, garden, or your indoor garden). Choose the most beautiful and vibrant plants. Touch the point of the white-handled knife gently to these in turn, forging a connection between your knife and the plants (and, thusly, the earth).

Next, sit on the earth. Ensuring that you are quite alone, draw a pentagram with the white-handled knife's point on the ground. It is done.

The Wand

If the wand is of wood, take it outdoors at sunset and rub it with fresh lavender, eucalyptus, or mint leaves. Raise it in the air toward the east (or the moon, if it is visible) and invoke the Goddess. At sunrise, take it again outdoors, rub with the fresh, fragrant leaves, and invoke the God by raising it to the east.

The Pentacle

Place the pentacle on bare earth. Lay upon it dried parsley, patchouli, mistletoe, or fresh jasmine or honeysuckle flowers. Sit before it facing north for several seconds, visualizing the pentacle absorbing the earth's energies. Then pick it up and scatter the herbs or flowers to the four quarters, beginning and ending in the north.

If this must be done indoors, fill a small dish with fresh earth and place the pentacle on this. Proceed as above, saving the herbs or flowers to be scattered outdoors at a later time.

The Censer

Fume pure rosemary, frankincense, or copal within the censer prior to its first use. Do this for about an hour.

The Cauldron

Take the cauldron to a stream, river, lake, or ocean. Gather the leaves of some plants growing nearby (at the sea, perhaps seaweed). Dip the cauldron into the water to fill it. Place the leaves in the cauldron, then set it on the water's edge where it is on both water and sand. Place your hands on the cauldron and dedicate it to the Goddess in any words you like. Empty and dry the cauldron, and return home. The charge has been made.

If performed inside, place the cauldron in a large basin of water or the bathtub, in a candle-lit room. Add a bit of salt to the water, which should be cold. Proceed as above.

Salt water corrodes metal. Thoroughly wash the cauldron after immersion in sea or salt water.

The Cup

Anoint the base with gardenia, rose, or violet oil and fill with pure spring water. Then set afloat a sprig of ivy, a small rose, a fresh gardenia, or some other appropriate flower or herb. Gaze into the cup and invoke the Goddess to bless it. You might also wish to take it outside at night, filled with water, and catch the moon's reflection within it.

The Broom

It can be fashioned from an ash staff, birch twigs, and a willow binding. Brush the broom with chamomile, willow, lemon balm, elder, or mallow stalks and branches, then bury these with due solemnity. You might also wish to carve a crescent moon upon its handle.

The Crystal

On the night of a full moon, rub the sphere with fresh (or dried) mugwort, then take it outside. Hold it up so that it drinks in the light and energies of the moon. Gaze at the moon through the crystal by holding it before your eyes. Repeat at least thrice yearly for the best benefits.

The Book of Shadows

Sew into the cover of the Book of Shadows leaves of the sacred herbs vervain, rue, bay, willow, or others, if you wish. They should be well-dried and secretly placed by the light of the moon. The covers of the Book of Shadows should, of course, be covered with cloth for this purpose.

The Robe

If you choose to wear one, lay it among sachets filled with lavender, vervain, and cedar when not in use. Sew a bit of rosemary or frankincense into the hem while fashioning it, if desired (and if any resulting stains won't show after washing).

Of the Herbs of the Sabbats

To be used as decorations on the altar, around the circle, in the home.

Samhain

Chrysanthemum, wormwood, apples, pears, hazel, thistle, pomegranates, all grains, harvested fruits and nuts, the pumpkin, and corn.

Yule

Holly, misteletoe, ivy, cedar, bay, juniper, rosemary, pine. Place offerings of apples, oranges, nutmegs, lemons, and whole cinnamon sticks on the Yule tree.

Imbolc

Snowdrop, rowan, the first flowers of the year.

Ostara

Daffodil, woodruff, violet, gorse, olive, peony, iris, narcissus; all spring flowers.

Beltane

Hawthorn, honeysuckle, St. John's wort, woodruff; all flowers.

Midsummer

Mugwort, vervain, chamomile, rose, lily, oak, lavender, ivy, yarrow, fern, elder, wild thyme, daisy, and carnation.

Lughnasadh

All grains, grapes, heather, blackberries, sloe, crab apples, and pears.

Mabon
Hazel, corn, aspen, acorns, oak sprigs, autumn leaves, wheat stalks, cypress cones, pine cones, and harvest gleanings.

Of the Herbs and Plants of Full Moon Rituals
Place upon the altar all nocturnal, white or five-petaled flowers such as the white rose, night-blooming jasmine, carnation, gardenia, cereus, lily, iris; all pleasingly scented flowers that shall call forth the Goddess. Camphor is also symbolic.

Of Offerings

To the Goddess
All watery and earthy flowers and seeds such as camellia, lily, water lily, willow stalks; those flowers used in full moon rituals; white or purple blooms such as hyacinth, magnolia, heather, and lilac; sweet-scented herbs and flowers; those dedicated to Venus or to the moon; rue, vervain, and olive; or others that seem suitable.

To the God
All fiery and airy herbs and flowers such as basil, chrysanthemum, snapdragon, clover, lavender, pine; strongly scented, clean, or citrusy herbs and flowers; those ruled by Mars or the sun; yellow or red blooms such as sunflower, pine cones, seeds, cacti, thistles, and stinging herbs; orange, heliotrope, cedar, juniper, and so on.

Of the Sacred Herbs of the Goddesses
Aphrodite: olive, cinnamon, daisy, cypress, quince, orris (iris), apple, myrtle

Aradia: rue, vervain

Artemis: silver fir, amaranth, cypress, cedar, hazel, myrtle, willow, daisy, mugwort, date palm

Astarte: alder, pine, cypress, myrtle, juniper

Athena: olive, apple

Bast: catnip, vervain

Bellona: belladonna

Brigit: blackberry

Cailleach: wheat

Cardea: hawthorn, bean, arbutus

Ceres: willow, wheat, bay, pomegranate, poppy, leek, narcissus

Cybele: oak, myrrh, pine

Demeter: wheat, barley, pennyroyal, myrrh, rose, pomegranate, bean, poppy, all cultivated crops

Diana: birch, willow, acacia, wormwood, dittany, hazel, beech, fir, apple, mugwort, plane, mulberry, rue

Druantia: fir

Freya: cowslip, daisy, primrose, maidenhair, myrrh, strawberry, mistletoe

Hathor: myrtle, sycamore, grape, mandrake, coriander, rose

Hecate: willow, henbane, aconite, yew, mandrake, cyclamen, mint, cypress, date palm, sesame, dandelion, garlic, oak, onion

Hekat: cypress

Hera: apple, willow, orris, pomegranate, myrrh

Hina: bamboo

Hulda: flax, rose, hellebore, elder

Irene: olive

Iris: wormwood, iris

Ishtar: acacia, juniper, all grains

Isis: fig, heather, wheat, wormwood, barley, myrrh, rose, palm, lotus, persea, onion, iris, vervain

Juno: lily, crocus, asphodel, quince, pomegranate, vervain, iris, lettuce, fig, mint

Kerridwen: vervain, acorns

Minerva: olive, mulberry, thistle

Nefer-tum: lotus

Nepthys: myrrh, lily

Nuit: sycamore

Olwen: apple

Persephone: parsley, narcissus, willow, pomegranate

Rhea: myrrh, oak

Rowen: clover, rowen

Venus: cinnamon, daisy, elder, heather, anemone, apple, poppy, violet, marjoram, maidenhair fern, carnation, aster, vervain, myrtle, orchid, cedar, lily, mistletoe, pine, quince

Vesta: oak

Of the Sacred Herbs of the Gods

Adonis: myrrh, corn, rose, fennel, lettuce, white heather

Aesculapius: bay, mustard

Ajax: delphinium

Anu: tamarisk

Apollo: leek, hyacinth, heliotrope, cornel, bay, frankincense, date palm, cypress

Attis: pine, almond

Ares: buttercup

Bacchus: grape, ivy, fig, beech, tamarisk

Baldur: St. John's wort, daisy

Bran: alder, all grains

Cupid: cypress, sugar, white violet, red rose

Dagda: oak

Dianus: fig

Dionysus: fig, apple, ivy, grape, pine, corn, pomegranate, toadstools, mushrooms, fennel, all wild and cultivated trees

Dis: cypress

Ea: cedar

Eros: red rose

Gwydion: ash

Helios: sunflower, heliotrope

Herne: oak

Horus: horehound, lotus, persea

Hypnos: poppy

Jove: pine, cassia, houseleek, carnation, cypress

Jupiter: aloe, agrimony, sage, oak, mullein, acorn, beech, cypress, houseleek, date palm, violet, gorse, ox-eye daisy, vervain

Kernunnos: heliotrope, bay, sunflower, oak, orange

Kanaloa: banana

Mars: ash, aloe, dogwood, buttercup, witch grass, vervain

Mercury: cinnamon, mulberry, hazel, willow

Mithras: cypress, violet

Neptune: ash, bladderwrack, all seaweeds

Odin: mistletoe, elm

Osiris: acacia, grape, ivy, tamarisk, cedar, clover, date palm, all grains

Pan: fig, pine, reed, oak, fern, all meadow flowers

Pluto: cypress, mint, pomegranate

Poseidon: pine, ash, fig, bladderwrack, all seaweeds

Prometheus: fennel

Ra: acacia, frankincense, myrrh, olive

Saturn: fig, blackberry

Sylvanus: pine

Tammuz: wheat, pomegranate, all grains

Thoth: almond

Thor: thistle, houseleek, vervain, hazel, ash, birch, rowan, oak, pomegranate, burdock, beech

Uranus: ash

Woden: ash

Zeus: oak, olive, pine, aloe, parsley, sage, wheat, fig

As the Wicca, we will take only that which we need from the green and growing things of the earth, never failing to attune with the plant before harvesting, nor failing to leave a token of gratitude and respect.

Here ends this herbal grimoire.

Wiccan Crystal Magic

CRYSTALS AND STONES are gifts of the Goddess and God. They are sacred, magical tools that can be used to enhance ritual and magic. Here are some of these ways of earth magic.

Preparing the Circle

The magic circle can be laid out with crystals and stones, if desired, rather than with herbs.

Beginning and ending in the north, lay 7, 9, 21, or 40 quartz crystals of any size around the circle, either inside the cord or in place of it. If the ritual to be conducted within the circle is of a usual spiritual or magical nature, place the quartz crystals with points outward. If of a protective nature, place with points facing inward.

If you use candles to mark the four quarters of the magic circle rather than large stones, ring each candle with any or all of the following stones:

North: moss agate, emerald, jet, olivine, salt, black tourmaline

East: imperial topaz, citrine, mica, pumice

South: amber, obsidian, rhodochrosite, ruby, lava, garnet

West: aquamarine, chalcedony, jade, lapis lazuli, moonstone, sugilite

A Stone Altar

To make this altar, search through dry river beds and seashores for a variety of smoothly shaped stones. Or check rock shops for appropriate pieces.

Create the altar itself of three large stones. Two smaller ones of even size are used as the base, while a longer, flat stone is placed on top of these to form the altar itself. On this place one stone to the left of the altar to represent the Goddess. This might be a natural, river-rounded stone, a holed stone, a quartz crystal sphere, or any of the stones related to the Goddess that are listed below.

To the right of the altar, place a stone to represent the God. This might be a piece of lava, a quartz crystal point, a long, thin, or club-shaped rock, or a God-symbolic stone such as those presented below.

Between these two stones place a smaller stone with a red candle affixed to it to represent the divine energy of the Goddess and God as well as the element of fire.

Before this, place a flat stone to receive offerings of wine, honey, cakes, semiprecious stones, flowers, and fruit.

A small, cupped stone (if one can be found) should be set to the left of the offering stone. Fill this with water to represent that element.

To the left of the offering stone place a flat rock. Pour salt upon this to symbolize the element of earth.

Additionally, another flat stone can be placed before the offering stone to serve as an incense burner.

Use a long, thin, terminated quartz crystal as a wand and a flint or obsidian arrowhead for the magic knife.

Any other tools that are needed can simply be placed on the altar. Or, try to find stone alternatives to them.

This setup can be used for all types of Wiccan rituals.

Stones of the Goddesses

In general, all pink, green, and blue stones; those related to the moon or Venus; water and earth-ruled stones, such as peridot, emerald, pink tourmaline, rose quartz, blue quartz, aquamarine, beryl, kunzite, and turquoise.

Stones that are related to specific deities follow.

Aphrodite: salt

Ceres: emerald

Coatlicue: jade

Cybele: jet

Diana: amethyst, moonstone, pearl

Freya: pearl

Great Mother, The: amber, coral, geodes, holed stones

Hathor: turquoise

Isis: coral, emerald, lapis lazuli, moonstone, pearl

Kwan Yin: jade

Lakshmi: pearl

Maat: jade

Mara: beryl, aquamarine

Nuit: lapis lazuli

Pele: lava, obsidian, peridot, olivine, pumice

Selene: moonstone, selenite

Tiamat: beryl

Venus: emerald, lapis lazuli, pearl

Stones of the God

Generally, all orange and red stones; stones related to the sun and Mars; fire and air-ruled stones, such as carnelian, ruby, garnet, orange calcite, diamond, tiger's eye, topaz, sunstone, bloodstone, red tourmaline.

Stones that are related to specific deities follow.

Aesculapius: agate

Apollo: sapphire

Bacchus: amethyst

Cupid: opal

Dionysius: amethyst

Mars: onyx, sardonyx

Neptune: beryl

Odin: holed stone

Poseidon: beryl, pearl,* aquamarine

Ra: tiger's eye

Tezcatlipoca: obsidian

---

* Pearl and coral have been mentioned in these lists as "stones" because they were anciently thought to be such. Our knowledge of them as products of living creatures leaves us with ethical questions of whether or not to use them in ritual. This must be a personal decision. Save for beach-gathered coral, I have chosen not to.

Cairns

In earlier times, throughout the world, people built mounds or piles of stones. These were sometimes formed to mark the passage of travelers, or to commemorate some historic event, but such cairns usually had ritual significance.

In magical thought, cairns are places of power. They concentrate the energies of the stones used to create them. Cairns are rooted in the earth but lift upward to the sky, symbolically representing the interconnectedness of the physical and spiritual realms.

During outdoor circles, a small cairn, composed of no more than nine or eleven rocks, can be fashioned at each point of the circle of stones. This can be done prior to creating the circle itself.

The next time you're in some wild, lonely place with a profusion of stones, clear a place among them and sit. Visualize a magical need. As you visualize, grasp a nearby stone. Feel the energy beating within it—the power of the earth, the power of nature. Place it on the cleared ground. Pick up another stone, still visualizing your need, and set it next to the first.

Still visualizing, continue to add stones, building them into a small pile. Keep adding stones until you feel them vibrating and pulsating before you. Place the last rock on top of the cairn with firm ritual intent—affirm to yourself, to the cairn, and to earth that with this final magical act you're manifesting your need.

Place your hands on either side of the pile. Give it your energy through your visualization. Nurse it. Feed it strength and see your need as being fulfilled.

Then leave the cairn alone to do its work.

A Quartz and Candle Spell

Have a candle of the color symbolic of your magical need, according to the following list (or as your intuition tells you):

White: protection, purification, peace

Red: protection, strength, health, passion, courage

Light blue: healing, patience, happiness

Dark blue: change, psychism

Green: money, fertility, growth, employment

Yellow: intellect, attraction, study, divination

Brown: healing animals

Pink: love, friendships

Orange: stimulation, energy

Purple: power, healing severe diseases, spirituation, meditation

With the tip of a cleansed, terminated quartz crystal, scratch a symbol of your need onto the candle. This might be a heart for love, a dollar sign for money, a fist for strength. Alternately, use an appropriate rune* or write your need on the candle with the crystal.

As you scratch or draw, visualize your need with crystal clarity as if it has already manifested. Place the candle in a holder. Set the crystal near it and light the wick. As the flame shines, again strongly visualize. The crystal, candle, and symbol will do their work.

* See the following section for runic information.

Symbols and Signs

)O(	The Goddess		Cup
	The God		Censer
	Candle		Pentacle
	Broom		Wand
	Cauldron		Magic Knife/Sword
	Balefire		Altar
	Widdershins		Deosil

Symbol	Meaning		Meaning	Symbol
	Herbs, Greens		Water	
	Wine		Immortality	
	Bane, Deadly, Poison		Salt	
	Magic Circle		The Moon	
	The Sun		Moonrise	
	Sunrise		Moonset	
	Sunset		Waxing Moon	
	Spring		Full Moon	
	Summer		Waning Moon	
	Autumn		New Moon	
	Winter			

Rune Magic

RUNES ARE SYMBOLS that, when drawn, painted, traced, carved, or visualized, release specific energies. As such, rune magic is surprisingly easy to practice and is undergoing a renaissance today.

In earlier times, runes were scratched onto birch bark, bone, or wood. They were carved onto weapons to ensure accurate shots, engraved on cups and goblets to ward off poisoning, and marked on goods and the home for protective purposes.

But much confusion surrounds these figures. Some feel that runes themselves contain hidden powers. The same is also said of the pentagram and other magical symbols. The thought here is that, simply by drawing a rune, the magician unleashes supernatural powers.

This isn't the case. Runes are tools of magic. *Their potency lies within their user.* If my neighbor happened to doodle a healing rune on a napkin and, later, used this to wipe his forehead, no healing energy would be transferred to him simply because he didn't put any into the rune.

Runes must be used with power to be magically effective. Carve, paint, or trace away—with visualization and with personal energy.

The ways to use runes are limited only by your imagination. For example, if a friend had asked me to speed her recovery from an illness, I might draw a healing rune on a plain piece of paper and sit before it.

While concentrating on the rune, I'd visualize my friend in a healed, whole state. Then, after building up personal power, I'd send the energy to her *in the shape of the rune.* I'd see it meshing with her body, unblocking, soothing, healing.

Or, I could carve the rune on a piece of cedar wood, again visualizing perfect health, and give it to her to wear.

Runes can also be fashioned onto food—with power—and then eaten to bring that specific energy back into the body; marked on the person with oil and visualization; carved onto a candle that is then burned to release its energies; traced or visualized in a pond or bathtub prior to entering it.

To draw runes on paper, specific ink colors related to each of the runes presented here can be found in their descriptions below, and can be utilized, if you wish. The colors work in harmony with the runes. Here are the runes:

The Runes

Good Fortune

This is an all-purpose rune, often used to close correspondence. It is also drawn on packages, inscribed on white candles to ensure fortune in all endeavors, or engraved onto jewelry.

Victory

Used in legal battles as well as in general-purpose magic. Inscribe on red candles while in the midst of battles of all sorts. Draw in scarlet ink and burn during ritual or carry with you.

Love

This is used not only to receive and strengthen love, but also to send love to a friend. Draw with emerald or pink ink, or visualize, engrave, and so on. May also be traced in pans of cooking food with a spoon or fork to infuse the food with loving vibrations.

Comfort

To bring relief and ease pain, and to send or induce happiness and comfort to others. If you're depressed or anxious, stand before a mirror, looking into your eyes, and visualize this rune embracing your body. Or, carve onto a pink candle and burn.

Wealth

Draw on your business card, if you have one. Visualize in your pocket, wallet, or purse. Trace with a money-attracting oil such as patchouli or cinnamon on paper money before spending to ensure its eventual return to you.

Possession

Represents tangible objects. Use as a symbol to obtain a needed item. For instance, if you need furniture for your house, this rune could be manipulated magically to represent all the needed items.

Travel

When you wish or need to travel, trace this rune on paper with yellow ink, visualizing yourself traveling to your desired destination. Wrap it around a feather and throw it off a high cliff or mail to your intended destination. Or, carve on a yellow candle, place the candle in its holder over a picture of the place you wish to visit, and burn the candle.

Fertility

If you wish to become fertile, trace this rune with oil or visualize it in the sexual region. Can also be used to induce mental fertility, and in most growth-type spells.

Physical Health

To improve or strengthen health. Visualize while exercising, dieting, and deep breathing.

Healing
Use to aid healing of the sick. It can be drawn in blue ink directly on pre-scriptions, visualized on medicines before taking, traced above or in herbal medicinal potions. This rune can also be made into a talisman and worn.

Orderliness
To maintain a structured life, or to keep thoughts in good order. Wear the rune or trace on the forehead.

Protection
This complex sign can be marked on the home, your car, or on any objects you wish safeguarded. Sewn or embroidered on clothing or robes, it offers personal protection. Can also be made into an amulet and worn or carried. In times of danger when you have no access to such amulets, visualize this rune strongly.

Protection
Another like the last.

A Man

Use in conjunction with other runes to represent the subject of the spell. For example, if I wake up and can't seem to get my thoughts together, I might draw this rune with power on a piece of paper in yellow ink to represent myself. Then I'd draw the orderliness rune directly on top of the man rune, while visualizing myself attaining this state.

A Woman

Another like the last. Use in conjunction with other runes for spells.

A Friendship

The man and woman runes can be drawn together for a variety of purposes; experiment.

Runic Spells

A Money Rune Spell

With clove or cinnamon oil, trace the money rune on the largest denomination bill you have. Put this in your wallet or purse and resist spending it for as long as possible. Every time you look at the bill, visualize the rune to reinforce its power. This will draw money to you.

A Rune Love Spell

On an orris root or a piece of apple wood, carve the rune for love. As you do so, visualize the type of person you wish to meet. Carry the rune with you for three days, placing it in your bed at night. On the evening of the third day, toss the root or wood into a river, stream, lake, spring, or ocean.

A Rune Petition

At your altar, take a piece of clean, white paper. Draw the rune appropriate to your need in the center of the paper. If you wish, add a pinch of herbs symbolic of your desire, or anoint the paper with an appropriate magical oil. Fold up the paper and hold it tightly while visualizing your need. Now take it to a fire and throw it on the flames. Or, light a red candle and hold the edge of the petition in the flame, then throw it into the cauldron or other heat-proof container to burn. If the paper isn't completely consumed by the flames, relight it and repeat the spell another day.

To Destroy Negativity or a Baneful Situation

Draw a rune representative of the negativity (disordered thoughts, war, poison—see below) on a piece of paper with black ink. Gaze at it, visualizing the baneful influence, habit, or situation. Then, all at once, blot the rune completely from sight with a jar of white ink or paint, completely destroying the rune. While the ink or paint dries, visualize a good fortune, orderliness, or comfort rune over the paper and blot out all thoughts of the problem.

Casting the Runes

As mentioned above, runes can be used to glimpse possible future events or unknown circumstances. Perhaps the oldest method entails marking each of the twelve runes below on flat wooden sticks or small branches of a tree (gathered, of course, with the collection formula in "An Herbal Grimoire," page 167). The rune sticks are held, the question or situation clearly visualized, and the sticks are cast to the ground.

Read the runes that are clearly visible. Or, with your eyes closed, pick out one rune stick at random. Divine its interpretation according to the above information, and then draw two more sticks at random, reading each as you take it from the pile on the floor.

Alternately, go to a riverbed, the beach, or a rock shop and collect twelve flat-sided stones. Draw or paint the runes on one side only of the stones. Visualize the question and cast the rune stones onto the floor. Interpret the runes on the stones that have landed faceup, reading them in a general order from right to left.

For example, the money rune next to "man" could signify that wealth will somehow come into your life connected with a man, or that money problems stem from a male influence. Interpretation of the stones relies heavily on your own intuitive and psychic powers, and the situation at hand.

Rune stones seem to have some built-in limitations. Most future readings cover a two-week period. Remember that as with all divinatory work, the runes show future *trends* only. If the picture they unfold for you is unappealing or dangerous, change your course to avoid such a future outcome.

The more you use rune stones, the more comfortable you will become with them. When not in use they can be placed in a basket, box, or cloth bag.

Here are twelve runes often used for divinatory purposes. You can also design your own runes and use them.

The Home: family relations, foundation, and stability. Self-image.

Possessions: tangible objects, the material world.

Love: emotional states, romance, spouse difficulties, or influences.

Poison: gossip, slander, negativity, baneful habits, harmful attitudes.

Wealth: money, financial concerns, employment, employers.

Disordered thoughts: emotional tension, irrationality, confusion, doubt.

Woman: a female influence, or a woman.

Man: a male influence, or a man.

Gift: legacies, promotions, windfalls; also physical gifts, psychic and spiritual gifts, sacrifices, volunteering, giving of oneself.

Comfort: ease, pleasure, security, happiness, joy, a turn for the better.

Death: the end of a matter, a new beginning, initiation, change in all forms, purification.

War: conflicts, quarrels, arguments, hostility, aggression, anger, confrontations.

Spells and Magic

Protective Chant

Visualize a triple circle of purplish light around your body while chanting:

I am protected by your might,
O gracious Goddess, day and night.

Another of the same type. Visualize a triple circle and chant:

Thrice around the circle's bound,
evil sink into the ground.

A Mirror Spell of Protection for the Home

Compose an altar. Place a censer in the center before an image of the Goddess. Have a twelve-inch (or so) round mirror there as well. Ring the altar with nine white candles. Burn a protective incense (such as sandalwood, frankincense, copal, or rosemary) in the censer.

Beginning with the candle most directly before the Goddess image, say these or similar words:

Lunar light protect me!

Repeat as you light each candle, until all are glowing. Now, holding the mirror, invoke the Goddess in her lunar aspect with these or similar words:

Great Goddess of the lunar light and mistress of the seas;
great Goddess of the mystic night
and of the mysteries;

within this place of candles bright
and with your mirror nigh;
protect me with your awesome might
while ill vibrations fly!

Standing before the altar, hold the mirror facing the candles so that it reflects their flames. Keeping the mirror toward the candles, move slowly, clockwise, around the altar, watching the reflected firelight bouncing off your surroundings.

Gradually increase your speed, mentally invoking the Goddess to protect you. Move faster and faster; watch the light shattering the air, cleansing it, burning away all negativity and all lines along which the ill energies have traveled into your home.

Charge your home with the protective light of the Goddess. Race around the candles until you've felt the atmosphere change, until you feel that your home has been cleansed and guarded by the Great Goddess.

When finished, stand once again before the image. Thank the Goddess in any words you wish. Pinch out the candles one by one, bind them together with white cord, and store them in a safe place until (and if) you need to use them again for this same purpose.

A Spell to Break the Powers of a Spell

If you believe that a spell has been cast against you, place a large black candle in a cauldron (or a large black bowl). The candle must be tall enough to extend a few inches above the cauldron's rim. Affix the candle to the bottom of the cauldron with warmed beeswax or the drippings of another black candle so that it will not tip over.

Fill the cauldron to the rim with fresh water, without wetting the candle's wick. An inch or two of the candle should remain above the water. Deep breathe, meditate, clear your mind, and light the candle. Visualize the suspected spell's power as residing within the candle's flame. Sit in quiet contemplation of the candle and visualize the power flowing and growing with the candle's flame (yes, the power against you). As the candle burns down, its flame will eventually sputter and go out as it contacts the water. As soon as the flame has been extinguished by the water, the spell will be dispersed.

Break your visualization of the spell's power; see it explode into dust, becoming impotent.

Pour the water into a hole in the ground, a lake, or stream. Bury the candle. It is done.

String Magic

Take cord, of the appropriate color, and shape it on the altar into a rune or the design of the object that you need: a car, a house, a paycheck. While you do this, visualize the needed object; raise power and send it forth to bring it to manifestation. So shall it be.

To Protect an Object
(from Morgana)

With the first and middle fingers, trace a pentagram over the object to be protected. Visualize electric-blue or purple flame streaming from your fingers to form the pentagram. Say this as you trace:

With this pentagram I lay
protection here both night and day.
And the one who should not touch
let his fingers burn and twitch.
I now invoke the law of three:
this is my will, so mote it be!

Appendix I
Occult Suppliers

THIS SMALL LISTING includes mail-order suppliers of Wiccan books, tools, devotional materials, music, herbs, candles and other items. Some catalogs are sent free; others require a small fee. Send a self-addressed, stamped envelope for information regarding catalog price (if any).

Many small businesses continue to appear. It's a good idea to peruse the latest issue of Llewellyn's *New Worlds* or *Circle Magazine* to find up-to-date mail-order listings.

CIRCLE Magazine
P.O. Box 9
Barneveld, WI 53507
www.circlesanctuary.org

Circle Sanctuary publishes *Circle Magazine,* formerly *Circle Network News,* a publication of interest to Wiccans and pagans of all persuasions. Circle Sanctuary also offers Wiccan music such as *Circle Magick Musick* by Selena Fox and Jim Alan. Circle Sanctuary is full of resources—check out their website.

The Crystal Cave
415 W. Foothill Blvd.
Claremont, CA 91711
(909) 626-0398

Ritual jewelry, candles, censers, crystals, incense, herbs, oils, charcoal blocks, cauldrons, and many other items.

Eye of the Cat
3314 E. Broadway
Long Beach, CA 90803
(562) 438-3569
eyeofthecat.org

Ritual tools and jewelry, herbs and oils, charcoal blocks, books, candles, crystals, incenses, Goddess and God images.

Isis Books and Gifts
5701 E. Colfax
Denver, CO 80220
(303) 321-0867
isisbooks.com

Ritual tools, candles, charcoal blocks, books, moon magic incenses and oils, crystals and stones, ritual jewelry.

Magickal Childe
35 W. 19th Street
New York, NY 10011
(212) 242-7182

Ritual tools, candles, charcoal blocks, books, incenses and oils, herbs, crystals and stones, Goddess and God images.

Magick Bookstore
2306 Highland Avenue
National City, CA 92050
(619) 477-5260

Athames and other ritual tools, herbs and oils, candles, incenses, books, ritual jewelry.

Mermade
3314 Palomino Lane
Las Vegas, NV 89107
Fax (702) 384-0595
www.heartmagic.com/mermade.html
Scrying mirrors, incenses, and oils.

Appendix II
Wiccan and Pagan Publications

As STATED BEFORE, solitary Wicca can be a lonely path, but it needn't be. Subscribing to such magazines and tabloids as the ones listed here is a way of connecting with others of like mind and of refreshing your spiritual experience. Additionally, many include contact ads or services to meet others of like mind.

Frequency of publication and subscription prices noted below were current as of this writing. Some changes may occur.

A great many Wiccan and Pagan publications are produced, so the list below is merely a sampling to get you started. The most complete guide to Wiccan groups is *Circle Guide to Pagan Groups*. It is published yearly by Circle Sanctuary and is $18. Visit www.circlesanctuary.org.

Happy reading and networking!

The Cauldron
Mike Howard Treforgan
Mansion Uangeodmor
Cardigan, Dyfed SA43 2LB
Wales, UK
www.the-cauldron.fsnet.co.uk/

A Welsh newsletter devoted to Wicca, Druidism, Odinism, and earth mysteries. I don't know how many issues are published each year, but the subscription rate is $28 annually in dollar bills only, no American checks. The editor asks that writers do not put "The Cauldron" on the envelope when addressing it to him.

CIRCLE Magazine
P.O. Box 9
Barneveld, WI 53507
www.circlesanctuary.org
(608) 924-2216

A publication devoted to Wicca, Shamanism, paganism, and earth mysteries. Rituals, invocations and incantations, herbcraft, contacts and reviews. Four issues annually, $19 sent bulk mail; $25 first-class mail.

The Unicorn
P.O. Box 8814
Minneapolis, MN 55408

Wicca, herbalism, shamanism. Write for information regarding subscription price.

Glossary

I'VE INCLUDED THIS glossary to provide easy access to definitions of some of the more obscure terms used in this book.

These are, of course, personal definitions, a reflection of my Wiccan involvement, and Wiccans may disagree with me on some small matters. This is to be expected, owing to our religion's individualistic structure. I've tried to make it as nonsectarian and universal as possible, however.

Italicized terms within the body of each discussion refer to other, related entries in the glossary.

Akasha: the fifth element, the omnipresent spiritual power that permeates the universe. It is the energy out of which the elements formed.

Amulet: a magically *charged* object that deflects specific, usually negative energies. Generally, a protective object. (Compare with *talisman*.)

Asperger: a bundle of fresh herbs or a perforated object used to sprinkle water during or preceding *ritual*, for purificatory purposes.

Athame: a Wiccan ritual knife. It usually has a double-edged blade and a black handle. The athame is used to direct *personal power* during *ritual* workings. It is seldom (if ever) used for actual, physical cutting. The term is of obscure origin, has many variant spellings among Wiccans, and an even greater variety of pronunciations. American East-Coast Wiccans may pronounce it as "Ah-THAM-ee" (to rhyme with "whammy"); I was first taught to say "ATH-ah-may" and later "ah-THAW-may." For various purposes currently unknown to me, I decided to substitute the term "magic knife" for athame in *The Standing Stones Book of Shadows*. Either term, or simply "knife," will do.

Balefire: a fire lit for magical purposes, usually outdoors. Balefires are traditional on *Yule, Beltane,* and *Midsummer.*

Bane: that which destroys life, which is poisonous, destructive, evil, dangerous.

Beltane: a Wiccan festival celebrated on April 30 or May 1 (traditions vary). Beltane is also known as May Eve, Roodmas, Walpurgis Night, Cethsamhain. Beltane celebrates the symbolic union, mat-ing, or marriage of the Goddess and God, and links in with the approaching summer months.

Besom: broom.

Bolline: the white-handled knife, used in magic and Wiccan ritual for practical purposes such as cutting herbs or piercing a pomegranate. Compare with *athame.*

Book of Shadows: a Wiccan book of rituals, spells, and magical lore. Once hand copied upon *initiation,* the Book of Shadows is now photocopied or typed in some *covens.* No one "true" Book of Shadows exists; all are relevant to their respective users.

Censer: a heat-proof container in which incense is smoldered. An incense burner. It symbolizes the element of air.

Charge, To: to infuse an object with *personal power.* "Charging" is an act of *magic.*

Circle, Magic. see *magic circle.*

Circle of Stones: see *magic circle.*

Conscious Mind: the analytical, materially based, rational half of our consciousness. The mind at work when we compute our taxes, theorize, or struggle with ideas. Compare with *psychic mind.*

Corn Dolly: a figure, often human-shaped, created by plaiting dried wheat or other grains. It represented the fertility of the earth and the Goddess in early European agricultural rituals and is still used in *Wicca*. Corn dollies aren't made from cobs or husks; corn originally referred to any grain other than maize and still does in most English-speaking countries except the United States.

Coven: a group of Wiccans, usually initiatory, and led by one or two leaders.

Craft, The: *Wicca. Witchcraft.* Folk magic.

Days of Power, The: see *sabbat.*

Deosil: clockwise, the direction of the sun's apparent motion in the sky. In Northern Hemisphere magic and religion, deosil movement is symbolic of life, positive energies, the "good." It is much-used in spells and rituals; i.e., "walk deosil around the circle of stones." Some Wiccan groups below the equator, notably in Australia, have switched from deosil to *widdershins* movements in their rituals, for the sun "moves" in an apparent counterclockwise motion from this vantage point. See also *widdershins.*

Divination: the magical art of discovering the unknown by interpreting random patterns or symbols through the use of tools such as clouds, tarot cards, flames, and smoke. Divination contacts the *psychic mind* by tricking or drowsing the *conscious mind* through *ritual* and observation or through manipulation of tools. Divination isn't necessary for those who can easily attain communication with the psychic mind, though they may practice it.

Divine Power: the unmanifested, pure energy that exists within the Goddess and God. The life force, the ultimate source of all things. Compare with *earth power* and *personal power.*

Earth Power: the energy that exists within stones, herbs, flames, wind, and other natural objects. It is manifested *divine power* and can be utilized during *magic* to create needed change. Compare with *personal power.*

Elements, The: earth, air, fire, and water. These four essences are the building blocks of the universe. Everything that exists (or that has potential to exist) contains one or more of these energies. The elements hum within ourselves and are also "at large" in the world. They can be utilized to cause change through *magic.* The four elements formed from the primal essence or power—*akasha.*

Esbat: a Wiccan ritual, usually occurring on the full moon.

Evocation: calling up spirits or other nonphysical entities, either to visible appearance or invisible attendance. Compare with *invocation.*

Grimoire: a magical workbook containing ritual information, formulae, magical properties of natural objects, and preparation of ritual equipment. Many of these works include "catalogs of spirits." The most famous of the old grimoires is probably *The Key of Solomon.** Most first appeared in the sixteenth and seventeenth centuries, though they may be far older and contain traces of Roman, Greek, Babylonian, late Egyptian, and Sumerian rites.

Handfasting: a Wiccan, pagan, or Gypsy wedding.

Imbolc: a Wiccan festival celebrated on February 2, also known as Candlemas, Lupercalia, Feast of Pan, Feast of Torches, Feast of the Waxing Light, Oimelc, Brigit's Day, and many other names. Imbolc celebrates the first stirrings of spring and the recovery of the Goddess from giving birth to the sun (the God) at *Yule.*

Initiation: a process whereby an individual is introduced or admitted into a group, interest, skill, or religion. Initiations may be ritual occasions but can also occur spontaneously.

Invocation: an appeal or petition to a higher power (or powers), such as the Goddess and God. A prayer. Invocation is actually a method of establishing conscious ties with those aspects of the Goddess and

---

* See Mathers, S. L. MacGregor in the "Magic" section of the bibliography.

God that dwell within us. In essence, then, we seemingly cause them to appear or make themselves known by becoming aware of them.

Kahuna: a practitioner of the old Hawaiian philosophical, scientific, and magical system.

Labrys: a double-headed axe that symbolized the Goddess in ancient Crete, still used by some Wiccans for this same purpose. The labrys may be placed on or leaned against the left side of the altar.

Lughnasadh: a Wiccan festival celebrated on August 1, also known as August Eve, Lammas, Feast of Bread. Lughnasadh marks the first harvest, when the fruits of the earth are cut and stored for the dark winter months, and when the God also mysteriously weakens as the days grow shorter.

Mabon: on or around September 21, the autumn equinox, Wiccans celebrate the second harvest. Nature is preparing for winter. Mabon is a vestige of ancient harvest festivals that, in some form or another, were once nearly universal among peoples of the earth.

Magic: the movement of natural energies (such as *personal power*) to create needed change. Energy exists within all things—ourselves, plants, stones, colors, sounds, movements. Magic is the process of rousing or building up this energy, giving it purpose, and releasing it. Magic is a natural, not supernatural, practice, though it is little understood.

Magic Circle, The: a sphere constructed of *personal power* in which Wiccan rituals are usually enacted. The term refers to the circle that marks the sphere's penetration of the ground, for it extends both above and below it. It is created through *visualization* and *magic*.

Magic Knife: see *athame*.

Meditation: reflection, contemplation, turning inward toward the self or outward toward *deity* or nature. A quiet time in which the practitioner may dwell upon particular thoughts or symbols, or allow them to come unbidden.

Megalith: a huge stone monument or structure. Stonehenge is perhaps the best-known example of megalithic construction.

Menhir: a standing stone probably lifted by early peoples for religious, spiritual, or magical reasons.

Midsummer: the summer solstice, usually on or near June 21, one of the Wiccan festivals and an excellent night for *magic*. Midsummer marks the point of the year when the sun is symbolically at the height of its powers, and so, too, the God. The longest day of the year.

Mighty Ones, The: beings, deities, or presences often *invoked* during Wiccan ceremony to witness or guard the rituals. The Mighty Ones are thought to be either spiritually evolved beings, once human, or spiritual entities created by or charged by the Goddess and God to protect the earth and to watch over the four directions. They are sometimes linked with the elements.

Neo-Pagan: literally, new-pagan. A member, follower, or sympathizer of one of the newly formed pagan religions now spreading throughout the world. All Wiccans are *pagan*, but not all pagans are Wiccan.

Old Ones, The: a Wiccan term often used to encompass all aspects of the Goddess and God. I've used it in this context in *The Standing Stones Book of Shadows*. Some Wiccans view it as an alternative of *The Mighty Ones*.

Ostara: occurring at the spring equinox, around March 21, Ostara marks the beginning of true, astronomical spring, when snow and ice make way for green. As such, it is a fire and fertility festival, celebrating the return of the sun, the God, and the fertility of the earth (the Goddess).

Pagan: from the Latin *paganus*, country-dweller. Today used as a general term for followers of Wicca and other magical, shamanistic, and polytheistic religions. Naturally, Christians have their own peculiar definition of this word. It can be interchanged with *neo-pagan*.

Pendulum: a divinatory device consisting of a string attached to a heavy object, such as a quartz crystal, root, or ring. The free end of the string is held in the hand, the elbow steadied against a flat surface, and a question is asked. The movement of the heavy object's swings determines the answer. A rotation indicates yes or positive energy. A back and forth swing signals the opposite. (There are many methods of deciphering the pendulum's movements; use those that work best for you.) It is a tool that contacts the *psychic mind*.

Pentacle: a ritual object (usually a circular piece of wood, metal, clay, etc.) upon which a five-pointed star *(pentagram)* is inscribed, painted, or engraved. It represents the *element* of earth. The words "pentagram" and "pentacle" are not interchangeable, though they understandably cause some confusion.

Personal Power: the energy that sustains our bodies. It ultimately originates from the Goddess and God (or, rather, the power behind them). We first absorb it from our biological mothers within the womb and, later, from food, water, the moon and sun, and other natural objects. We release personal power during stress, exercise, sex, conception, and childbirth. Magic is often a movement of personal power for a specific goal.

Polarity: the concept of equal, opposite energies. The eastern yin/yang is a perfect example. Yin is cold; yang is hot. Other examples of polarity: Goddess/God, night/day, moon/sun, birth/death, dark/light, *psychic mind/conscious mind*. Universal balance.

Projective Hand, The: the hand that is normally used for manual activities such as writing, peeling apples, and dialing telephones is symbolically thought to be the point at which *personal power* is sent from the body. In ritual, personal power is visualized as streaming out from the palm or fingers of the hand for various magical goals. This is also the hand in which tools such as the *athame* and wand are held. Ambidextrous persons simply choose which hand to utilize for this purpose. Compare with *receptive hand*.

Psychic Mind: the subconscious or unconscious mind, in which we receive psychic impulses. The psychic mind is at work when we sleep, dream, and meditate. It is our direct link with the Goddess and God and with the larger, nonphysical world around us. Other related terms: *divination* is a ritual process which utilizes the *conscious mind* to contact the psychic mind. *Intuition* is a term used to describe psychic information that unexpectedly reaches the conscious mind.

Psychism: the act of being consciously psychic, in which the *psychic mind* and *conscious mind* are linked and working in harmony. *Ritual consciousness* is a form of psychism.

Receptive Hand: the left hand in right-handed persons, the reverse for left-handed persons. This is the hand through which energy is received into the body. Compare with *projective hand*.

Reincarnation: the doctrine of rebirth. The process of repeated incarnations in human form to allow evolution of the sexless, age-less soul.

Ritual: ceremony. A specific form of movement, manipulation of objects, or inner processes designed to produce desired effects. In religion, ritual is geared toward union with the divine. In *magic* it produces a specific state of consciousness that allows the magician to move energy toward needed goals. A *spell* is a magical ritual.

Ritual Consciousness: a specific, alternate state of awareness necessary to the successful practice of *magic*. The magician achieves this through the use of *visualization* and *ritual*. It denotes a state in which the *conscious mind* and *psychic mind* are attuned, in which the magician senses energies, gives them purpose, and releases them toward the magical goal. It is a heightening of the senses, an awareness-expansion of the seemingly nonphysical world, a linking with nature and with the forces behind all conceptions of *deity*.

Runes: stick-like figures, some of which are remnants of old Teutonic alphabets. Others are pictographs. These symbols are once again widely being used in *magic* and *divination*.

Sabbat: a Wiccan festival. See *Beltane, Imbolc, Lughnasadh, Mabon, Midsummer, Ostara, Samhain,* and *Yule* for specific descriptions.

Samhain: a Wiccan festival celebrated on October 31, also known as November Eve, Hallowmas, Halloween, Feast of Souls, Feast of the Dead, Feast of Apples. Samhain marks the symbolic death of the sun God and his passing into the "land of the young," where he awaits rebirth of the Mother Goddess at *Yule*. This Celtic word is pronounced by Wiccans as: SOW-wen; SEW wen; SAHM-hain; SAHM-ain; SAV-een, and other ways. The first seems to be the one preferred among most Wiccans.

Scry, To: to gaze at or into an object (a quartz crystal sphere, pool of water, reflections, a candle flame) to still the *conscious mind* and to contact the *psychic mind*. This allows the scryer to become aware of possible events prior to their actual occurrence, as well as of previous or distant, simultaneous events through other than the normally accepted senses. A form of *divination*.

Shaman: a man or woman who has obtained knowledge of the subtler dimensions of the earth, usually through periods of alternate states of consciousness. Various types of *ritual* allow the shaman to pierce the veil of the physical world and to experience the realm of energies. This knowledge lends the shaman the power to change her or his world through *magic*.

Shamanism: the practice of shamans, usually ritualistic or magical in nature, sometimes religious.

Simple Feast, The: a *ritual* meal shared with the Goddess and God.

Spell: a magical *ritual*, usually nonreligious in nature and often accompanied by spoken words.

Spirits of the Stones, The: the elemental energies naturally inherent at the four directions of the *magic circle*, personified within the *Standing Stones Tradition* as the "spirits of the stones." They are linked with the *elements*.

Talisman: an object, such as an amethyst crystal, ritually *charged* with power to attract a specific force or energy to its bearer. Compare with *amulet*.

Tradition, Wiccan: an organized, structured, specific Wiccan subgroup, usually initiatory, with often unique ritual practices. Many traditions have their own *Books of Shadows* and may or may not recognize members of other traditions as Wiccan. Most traditions are composed of a number of *covens* as well as solitary practitioners.

Trilithon: a stone arch made from two upright slabs with one lying atop these. Trilithons are featured in Stonehenge as well as the circle visualization in *The Standing Stones Book of Shadows.*

Visualization: the process of forming mental images. Magical visualization consists of forming images of needed goals during *ritual.* Visualization is also used to direct *personal power* and natural energies during *magic* for various purposes, including *charging* and forming the *magic circle.* It is a function of the *conscious mind.*

White-Handled Knife: a normal cutting knife, with a sharp blade and white handle. It is used within *Wicca* to cut herbs and fruits, to slice bread during *The Simple Feast,* and for other functions—but never for sacrifice. Sometimes called the bolline. Compare with *athame.*

Wicca: a contemporary *pagan* religion with spiritual roots in *shamanism* and the earliest expressions of reverence of nature. Among its major motifs are: reverence for the Goddess and the God; reincarnation; magic; ritual observances of the full moon, astronomical and agricultural phenomena; spheroid temples, created with *personal power,* in which rituals occur.

Widdershins: anticlockwise motion, usually used in the Northern Hemisphere for negative magical purposes or for dispersing negative energies or conditions such as disease. Southern Hemisphere Wiccans may use widdershins motions for exactly the opposite purposes; namely for positive ends, for the reason stated in the entry under *deosil.* In either case, widdershins and deosil motions are *symbolic;* only strict, closed-minded traditionalists believe that accidentally walking around the altar backward, for instance, will raise negativity. Their use in Wicca stems from ancient European rituals practiced by peoples who watched and reverenced the sun and moon in their daily revolutions. Widdershins motion, within ritual contexts, is still shunned by the vast majority of Wiccans, though others use it once in a while, for instance, to disperse the *magic circle* at the end of a rite.

Witch: anciently, a European practitioner of the remnants of pre-Christian folk magic, particularly that relating to herbs, healing, wells, rivers, and stones. One who practiced *Witchcraft*. Later, this term's meaning was deliberately altered to denote demented, dangerous, supernatural beings who practiced destructive magic and who threatened Christianity. This change was a political, monetary, and sexist move on the part of organized religion, not a change in the practices of Witches. This later, erroneous meaning is still accepted by many non-Witches. It is also, somewhat surprisingly, used by some members of *Wicca* to describe themselves.

Witchcraft: the *craft* of the *Witch—magic,* especially magic utilizing *personal power* in conjunction with the energies within stones, herbs, colors and other natural objects. While this may have spiritual overtones, Witchcraft, using this definition, isn't a religion. Some followers of Wicca use this word to denote their religion, however.

Yule: a *Wiccan* festival celebrated on or about December 21, marking the rebirth of the sun God from the earth Goddess. A time of joy and celebration during the miseries of winter. Yule occurs on the winter solstice.

Suggested Reading

THIS IS A WIDE-ranging list of books related, in some way, to Wicca. A book's inclusion here doesn't necessarily indicate that I'm in perfect agreement with its contents. Many of these books were written from far different perspectives than the one you've been reading.

All, however, if read with intelligence and discrimination, will deepen your understanding of the Goddess and God, and of the myriad forms of Wicca, magic, and shamanism.

Those asterisked (*) are highly recommended.

Where I felt it important, I have appended short comments concerning the book's contents, *not* my views on them.

Such a list as this cannot hope to be complete. Books on these subjects are being published every day. Still, this should serve as a starting point for those interested in reading further.

Shamanism

Lynn V. *Medicine Woman.* San Francisco: Harper & Row, 1981.

Bend, Cynthia, and Tayja Wiger. *Birth of a Modern Shaman.* St. Paul: Llewellyn Publications, 1988.

Castaneda, Carlos. *The Teachings of Don Juan: A Yaqui Way of Knowledge.* New York: Ballantine, 1970.

Furst, Peter T. *Hallucinogens and Culture.* Corte Madera (California): Chandler & Sharp Publishers, 1976.

*Harner, Michael J. (editor). *Hallucinogens and Shamanism.* New York: Oxford University Press, 1978.

*Harner, Michael. *The Way of the Shaman.* San Francisco: Harper & Row, 1981. The first "how-to" book on this subject, *The Way of the Shaman* introduces simple techniques for acquiring alternate states of consciousness, on contacting your power animal, healing rituals, and much else of interest.

*Howells, William. *The Heathens: Primitive Man and His Religions.* Garden City (New York): Doubleday, 1956. Covers the entire range of pre–Christian and pre-technological religion and magic, including totemism, ancestor worship, shamanism, divination, mana, and tabu.

Kilpatrick, Jack Frederick, and Anna Gritts. *Notebook of a Cherokee Shaman.* Washington D.C.: Smithsonian, 1970.

Deer, John (Fire), and Richard Erdoes. *Lame Deer: Seeker of Visions.* New York: Pocket Books, 1978. A portrait of a contemporary shaman, revealing the essential humanness of the subject. Much Sioux lore.

Lewis, I. M. *Ecstatic Religion: an Anthropological Study of Spirit Possession and Shamanism.* Baltimore: Penquin, 1976. This is a scholarly sociological investigation into shamanism and alternate states of consciousness.

Rogers, Spencer L. *The Shaman's Healing Way.* Ramona (California): Acoma Books, 1976.

*Sharon, Douglas. *Wizard of the Four Winds: A Shaman's Story.* New York: The Free Press, 1978. A portrait of Eduardo Calderon, a contemporary Peruvian shaman, detailing much of his rites and rituals.

*Torrey, E. Fuller. *The Mind Game: Witchdoctors and Psychiatrists.* New York: Bantam, 1973.

*Wellman, Alice. *Spirit Magic.* New York: Berkeley, 1973. This short paperback is a guide to shamanism as practiced in various parts of the world. One chapter, "The Tools of Wizardry," is of particular interest.

Goddess Studies

Briffault, Robert. *The Mothers.* (Abridged by Gordon Taylor.) New York: Atheneum, 1977.

Downing, Christine. *The Goddess: Mythological Images of the Feminine.* New York: Crossroad, 1984.

*Graves, Robert. *The White Goddess.* New York: Farrar, Straus and Giroux, 1973. Perhaps the book that has had the greatest effect on modern Wicca. A poetic investigation into the Goddess.

*Harding, Esther. *Women's Mysteries: Ancient and Modern.* New York: Pantheon, 1955.

James, E. O. *The Cult of the Mother-Goddess.* New York: Barnes and Noble, 1959.

Leland, Charles G. *Aradia, or the Gospel of the Witches.* New York: Buckland Museum, 1968. This work presents a very different view of the Goddess than most others. The material was collected by Mr. Leland in the late 1800s and has had an affect on current Wicca.

*Newmann, Erich. *The Great Mother: an Analysis of the Archetype.* Princeton: Princeton University Press, 1974. A Jungian approach to the Goddess. This book concludes with 185 pages of photographs of Goddess images.

Stone, Merlin. *When God Was a Woman.* New York: Dial Press, 1976.

Walker, Barbara. *The Women's Encyclopedia of Myths and Mysteries.* San Francisco: Harper & Row, 1983.

Folklore, Mythology, Legend and History

*Bord, Janet, and Colin Bord. *Earth Rites: Fertility Practices in Pre-Industrial Britain.* London: Granada, 1982. An account of pagan rituals of Britain.

Busenbark, Ernest. *Symbols, Sex and the Stars in Popular Beliefs.* New York: Truth Seeker, 1949.

*Campbell, Joseph. *The Masks of God: Creative Mythology.* New York: Viking Press, 1971.

———. *The Masks of God: Oriental Mythology.* New York: Viking Press, 1977.

———. *The Masks of God: Primitive Mythology.* New York: Viking Press, 1977. These books cover the whole sweep of worldwide mythology.

———. *Myths to Live By.* New York: Bantam Books, 1973.

*Carpenter, Edward. *Pagan and Christian Creeds: Their Origin and Meaning.* New York: Harcourt, Brace and Company, 1920. An early work by a renegade scholar, it shows the origins of many Christian religious symbols from earlier pagan religions. Along the way it covers food and vegetation magic, pagan initiations, ritual dancing, the sex-taboo, and much else of interest.

*Dexter, T. F. G. *Fire Worship in Britain.* London: Watts and Co., 1931. A forty-three-page booklet, printed before World War II, detailing the survivals of ancient pagan festivals in Britain before that conflict ended many of them forever.

*Enrenreich, Barbara, and Deirdre English. *Witches, Midwives and Nurses: a History of Women Healers.* Old Westbury (New York): 1973. An important investigation of the role of women as healers and witches in earlier times.

Frazer, Sir James. *The Golden Bough.* New York: Macmillan, 1956. (One volume abridged edition.)

Harley, Timothy. *Moon Lore.* Tokyo: Charles E. Tuttle Co., 1970.

Kenyon, Theda. *Witches Still Live.* New York: Washburn, 1929. An early collection of myths, legends, and tales of Witches and folk magicians.

*Leach, Maria (editor), and Jerome Fried (associate editor). *Funk and Wagnall's Standard Dictionary of Folklore, Mythology and Legend.* New York: Funk and Wagnall's, 1972. This classic, one-volume collection nearly sums up the totality of mythic information. Of great interest to Wiccans.

Watts, Alan. *The Two Hands of God: the Myths of Polarity.* New York: Coffier, 1978.

Wentz, W. Y. Evans. *The Fairy-Faith in Celtic Countries.* London: Oxford University Press, 1911. Gerrards Cross (Buckinghamshire, England): 1981.

Wicca

Bowness, Charles. *The Witch's Gospel.* London: Robert Hale, 1979.

Buckland, Raymond. *Witchcraft . . . The Religion.* Bay Shore (New York): The Buckland Museum of Witchcraft and Magick, 1966. An early explication of Gardnerian Wicca.

Buczynski, Edmund M. *The Witchcraft Fact Book.* New York: Magickal Childe, n.d.

Crowther, Patricia. *Witch Blood! The Diary of a Witch High Priestess.* New York: House of Collectibles, 1974.

Deutch, Richard. *The Ecstatic Mother: Portrait of Maxine Sanders— Witch Queen.* London: Bachman and Turner, 1977. One of the key figures of the Alexandrian Wiccan tradition is explored in this work.

*Gardner, Gerald. *The Meaning of Witchcraft.* London: 1959. London: Aquarian Press, 1971. An historical look at Wicca.

———. *Witchcraft Today.* New York: Citadel, 1955. The first book written about contemporary Wicca details what has come to be termed Gardnerian Wicca.

*Glass, Justine. *Witchcraft: the Sixth Sense and Us.* North Hollywood: Wilshire, 1965.

Johns, June. *King of the Witches: the World of Alex Sanders.* New York: Coward McCann, 1969. Another investigation of Alexandrian Wicca and a biography of its founder.

Lady Sara. *Questions and Answers on Wicca Craft.* Wolf Creek (Oregon): Stonehenge Farm, 1974.

*Leek, Sybil. *The Complete Art of Witchcraft.* New York: World Publishing, 1971. This influential work describes an eclectic Wiccan tradition.

———. *Diary of a Witch.* New York: Prentice-Hall, 1968.

"Lugh." *Old George Pickingill and the Roots of Modern Witchcraft.* London: Wiccan Publications, 1982. Taray, 1984. This work purports to describe the historical background to the modern revival of Wicca by Gerald Gardner.

Martello, Leo L. *Witchcraft: the Old Religion.* Secaucus: University Books, 1974. An investigation into Sicilian Wicca.

Roberts, Susan. *Witches USA.* New York: Dell, 1971. Hollywood: Phoenix, 1974. This book, an investigation into Wicca by an outsider, created a storm of controversy when it was reprinted. It stands as an overview of part of the Wiccan scene circa 1970, and is no more flawed by inaccuracies than any other book included in this list.

Sanders, Alex. *The Alex Sanders Lectures.* New York: Magickal Childe, 1980. Another look at Alexandrian Wicca.

Sanders, Maxine. *Maxine the Witch Queen.* London: Star Books, 1976. Yet another look—this time autobiographical—at the founding and activities of Alexandrian Wicca.

*Valiente, Doreen. *An ABC of Witchcraft Past and Present.* New York: St. Martin's, 1973. A Gardnerian Wiccan's answer to earlier Witchcraft books, this is an encyclopedic look at British Wicca, folklore, and legend.

*———. *Where Witchcraft Lives.* London: Aquarian Press, 1962. An early look at British Wicca and Sussex folklore.

Practical Instructions

*Alan, Jim, and Selena Fox. *Circle Magic Songs.* Madison (Wisconsin): Circle Publications, 1977.

Budapest, Z. *The Feminist Book of Light and Shadows.* Venice (California): Luna Publications, 1976. An influential, first book of feminist Wicca.

———. *The Holy Book of Women's Mysteries Part I.* Oakland: The Susan B. Anthony coven #1, 1979. An expanded version of the above book. A second volume was also published.

Buckland, Raymond. *The Tree: The Complete Book of Saxon Witchcraft.* New York: Weiser, 1974.

*———. *Buckland's Complete Book of Witchcraft.* St. Paul: Llewellyn Publications, 1985 and 2002. A course in Wicca, drawn from several traditions. Includes a section on solitary practitioners.

Crowther, Patricia. *Lid Off the Cauldron: A Wicca Handbook.* London: Robert Hale, 1981. Another how-to book.

*Farrar, Janet and Stewart Farrar. *Eight Sabbats for Witches.* London: Robert Hale, 1981. These once-Alexandrian Wiccans have explored new territory, incorporating much Irish lore and deity-forms. This book also presents a unique look at the origins of the so-called Gardnerian Book of Shadows.

*———. *The Witches' Way: Principles, Rituals and Beliefs of Modern Witchcraft.* London: Robert Hale, 1984. Further revelations concerning Gardner's Book of Shadows and much practical information.

*Fitch, Ed. *Magical Rites From the Crystal Well.* St. Paul: Llewellyn Publications, 1984. A collection of neo-pagan rituals for every occasion.

K., Amber. *How to Organize a Coven or Magical Study Group.* Madison (Wisconsin): Circle Publications, 1983. Guidelines for doing just that.

*Slater, Herman (editor). *A Book of Pagan Rituals.* New York: Weiser, 1974. Another collection of rituals, this time drawn from the Pagan Way.

*Starhawk. *The Spiral Dance: a Rebirth of the Ancient Religion of the Great Goddess.* San Francisco: Harper and Row, 1979. It seems strange that it's been nearly ten years since this book was first published. It has had a tremendous impact on Wiccan groups and individuals. Definitely Goddess- and woman-oriented, it includes exercises for developing magical fluency and many rituals as well.

Valiente, Doreen. *Witchcraft for Tomorrow.* London: Robert Hale, 1978. Valiente's work, the first of the modern how-to-practice-Wicca books, contains a complete Book of Shadows, which she wrote just for publication, as well as several chapters covering various aspects of Wicca.

*Weinstein, Marion. *Earth Magic: A Dianic Book of Shadows.* New York: Earth Magic Productions, 1980. This is a Wiccan book like no other. It contains complete, explicit information on forming alignments with "all five aspects" of the deities, working with familiars, the tools, and much else of interest. An expanded version has been published.

Spell Books

Buckland, Raymond. *Practical Candleburning Rituals.* St. Paul: Llewellyn Publications, 1971.

*Chappel, Helen. *The Waxing Moon: A Gentle Guide to Magic.* New York: Links, 1974.

Dixon, Jo and James. *The Color Book: Rituals, Charms and Enchantments.* Denver: Castle Rising, 1978.

Grammary, Ann. *The Witch's Workbook.* New York: Pocket, 1973.

Huson, Paul. *Mastering Witchcraft*. New York: Berkeley, 1971. An early book responsible, in part, for the tremendous interest in occult matters during the early 1970s. Little of its information bears much resemblance to Wicca, or to the type of magic Wiccans practice.

Lorde, Simon, and Clair Lorde. *The Wiccan Guide to Witches Ways*. New South Wales (Australia): K J. Forrest, 1980.

Malbrough, Ray T. *Charms, Spells and Formulas for the Making and Use of Gris-Gris, Herb Candles, Doll Magick, Incenses, Oils and Powders to Gain Love, Protection, Prosperity, Luck and Prophetic Dreams*. St. Paul: Llewellyn, 1986. A collection of Cajun magic from Louisiana.

Paulsen, Kathryn. *Witches Potions and Spells*. Mount Vernon: Peter Pauper Press, 1971.

*Worth, Valerie. *The Crone's Book of Words*. St. Paul: Llewellyn Publications, 1971, 1986.

Agrippa, Henry Cornelius. *The Philosophy of Natural Magic*. Antwerp, 1531. Secaucus: University Books, 1974. This is the first of the three books mentioned in the next entry.

*———. *Three Books of Occult Philosophy*. London: 1651. London: Chthonios Books, 1986. This book constituted the bulk of magical information known in the sixteenth century. Stones, stars, herbs, incenses, sigils, and all manner of delights are to be found in this book. Recently reprinted in its entirety for the first time in three hundred years.

*Baneft, Francis. *The Magus, or Celestial Intelligencer, Being a Complete System of Occult Philosophy*. 1801. New Hyde Park (New York): University Books, 1967. Ceremonial (as opposed to natural) magic.

*Burland, C. A. *The Magical Arts: A Short History*. New York: Horizon Press, 1966. A history of folk magic.

Devine, M. V. *Brujeria: A Study of Mexican-American Folk-Magic*. St. Paul: Llewellyn Publications, 1982.

Fortune, Dion. *Psychic Self-Defence.* London: Aquarian, 1967.

*Howard, Michael. *The Magic of Runes.* New York: Weiser, 1980.

————. *The Runes and Other Magical Alphabets.* New York: Weiser, 1978.

Koch, Rudolph. *The Book of Signs.* New York: Dover, 1955. A book of signs, symbols, and runes.

Leland, Charles Godfrey. *Etruscan Magic and Occult Remedies.* New Hyde Park (New York): University Books, 1963.

————. *Gypsy Sorcery and Fortune-Telling.* New York: Dover, 1971.

Mathers, S. L MacGregor (editor and translator). *The Key of Solomon the King.* New York: Weiser, 1972.

*Mickaharic, Draja. *Spiritual Cleansing: A Handbook of Psychic Protection.* York Beach (Maine): Weiser, 1982. Some of the magic in this work is shamanistic in tone and origin.

*Pepper, Elizabeth, and John Wilcox. *Witches All.* New York: Grosset and Dunlap, 1977. A collection of folk magic drawn from the popular (now defunct) Witches Almanac.

Pliny the Elder. *Natural History.* Cambridge: Harvard University Press, 1956.

Shah, Sayed Idries. *Oriental Magic.* New York: Philosophical Library, 1957.

————. *The Secret Lore of Magic.* New York: Citadel, 1970. Extracts from several Renaissance books of ceremonial magic.

————. *Occultism: Its Theory and Practice.* Castle Books. n.d.

Valiente, Doreen. *Natural Magic.* New York: St. Martin's Press, 1975.

*Weinstein, Marion. *Positive Magic: Occult Self-Help.* New York: Pocket Books, 1978. An introduction to magic. An expanded edition of this popular book has also been published.

Periodicals Consulted

Some of these magazines and newspapers are still being published; others are not:

A Pagan Renaissance

Circle Network News

The Crystal Well

Earth Religions News

Georgian Newsletter

Gnostica

The Green Egg

Nemeton

The New Broom

New Dimensions

Pentagram

Revival

Seax-Wicca Voys

The Unicorn

The Waxing Moon

The Witch's Almanac

Index

Llewellyn.com is friendly, easy to use, and more interactive than ever.

- Online bookstore where you can browse inside our books

- Special offers and discounts

- Astrology readings

- Free web tarot readings

- Free e-newsletters

- Author interviews and upcoming events

- Recipes, tips, and spells

- Moon phases

- Spell-a-day

- Llewellyn encyclopedia

- Articles by your favorite authors

- Blogs on the topics you care about

www.llewellyn.com

Get Social with Llewellyn

Find us on facebook. • Follow us on twitter
www.Facebook.com/LlewellynBooks • www.Twitter.com/Llewellynbooks